THE CONFLUENT SPEAKER

A FRAMEWORK TO BUILD CONFIDENCE & FLUENCY IN ENGLISH

ZIAUR REHMAN

Contents

SECTION I: MINDSET

Contents

SECTION II: KNOWLEDGE

SECTION III: PRACTICE

SECTION IV: FEEDBACK

THE ROAD AHEAD FOR YOU AS A CONFLUENT SPEAKER

Why I Wrote This Book

Let me be upfront with you: this is not a research-based book, and I'm not a certified author with some grand academic qualification. Sure, I have a Master's degree in English, but let me tell you, I did not get top grades. In fact, after completing my master's, I didn't even bother to check my final results. It's still sitting there, somewhere in the system. I may go check it someday, but honestly, I'm not bothered. I've been coaching for over 10 years now, and not once has anyone asked me about my grades or my college degree.

I didn't even start my journey as a teacher in the traditional sense. I wasn't born with a plan to become an English coach. In fact, I worked as a waiter for several years before I ever thought about teaching. Random jobs, meeting different people, working at weddings and parties—I had no plan of becoming an English teacher. I came from a Hindi-medium school, so my foundation was in a completely different environment. But one day, I got an opportunity to step into coaching, and that's when things started to change.

Through my experiences working with all sorts of people—builders, politicians, engineers, designers, artists, even musicians—I've had the privilege of learning from many different walks of life. This book is not just a product of my studies; it's a reflection of my real-world experiences, of the gaps I've noticed time and time again in how English is taught and learned.

The truth is, the language learning system in India focuses too much on rules and not enough on real conversations. People want to speak confidently, but they're often told grammar is the only thing that matters. But it's not just about knowing rules. It's about knowing how to use the language in real life. It's about your mindset, your knowledge, your practice, and your ability to receive feedback. That's why I created the MKPF framework.

This book is a guide to becoming a **Confluent Speaker**—someone who is not just fluent, but confident in speaking English in any setting. Whether you're talking in a group of 5 or speaking up at a meeting or social gathering, this book will help you understand the areas of language that matter most and give you the tools to build your confidence.

But let me clarify: this book isn't about writing skills. If you're looking for a guide to become a better writer, this book may not be for you. But if you're looking to improve your speaking skills and connect more confidently with people, you're in the right place. I designed this book specifically for **speaking**—whether you're speaking in public or simply having a conversation with friends, family, or colleagues.

If you're looking for a research-heavy, academic book with references and citations, you won't find that here.

I'm not claiming to be an academic expert. I don't have a fancy degree from some prestigious institution. I'm just someone who's been in the trenches for over a decade, working with real people, facing real challenges. And through that, I've learned what works. I've learned what helps people go from simply knowing English to **being able to speak it confidently** in real-life situations.

And I don't want you to think of this as some perfect, polished work either. This book is a reflection of my personal journey. It's me putting out my thoughts, experiences, and the things I've learned over the years. It's not about being the best book or the final word on language learning; it's about starting a conversation—one that I hope will help you find your path to fluency and confidence.

So, if you connect with my story, with the way I approach learning and teaching, then this book is for you. If you're looking for something more academic or structured, you might want to look elsewhere. But if you want something real, something practical, something that comes from years of teaching and coaching people just like you, then keep reading. This is not about being certified by society's standards. It's about being real and finding your own voice, just like I did.

I'm here to guide you—not with fancy degrees or titles, but with the belief that everyone, no matter where they start, has the potential to speak confidently and fluently. **Independence** is the goal. This book is your starting point to **becoming independent** in your learning.

What Does It Mean to Be Confluent?

Have you ever found yourself hesitating to speak in English because you feared making mistakes? Have you ever thought, *"I'll speak confidently when I'm perfect"*?

If yes, let me tell you something important: **perfection is not the goal—progress is.**

For years, learners have been told that fluency is about perfect grammar, big words, and sounding like a native speaker. But I have discovered something different through my work with people from all walks of life— lawyers, artists, professionals, students. Fluency without confidence is incomplete. You need both.

That's why I created the term **Confluent.** It is not just a word. It is an identity.

Confluent = Confident + Fluent

A *Confluent Speaker* expresses themselves naturally and effectively in English—not flawlessly, but **fearlessly.**

Let's be honest: mistakes are a part of growth. A Confluent Speaker doesn't shy away from conversations; they embrace them as opportunities to connect, learn, and improve.

This book is built around this idea. Every chapter, every exercise, and every story will help you build confidence alongside fluency. You are not starting from zero. You already have some degree of fluency, and together, we will strengthen it step by step.

Why "Confluent"?

I created the term *Confluent* because traditional labels like "fluent" or "proficient" don't capture the whole journey of becoming an effective speaker. People often measure fluency as a destination—a perfect state where they never make mistakes. But in reality, fluency is a process, and confidence plays a vital role in that process.

Being a *Confluent Speaker* means:

- You're not aiming for perfection; you're aiming for connection.

- You're aware of your current abilities and working on your growth every day.

- You speak with authenticity, knowing that the real goal is to communicate effectively, not flawlessly.

This term shifts the focus from rigid linguistic standards to a more holistic approach—embracing the speaker's mindset, their practical skills, and their ability to engage in meaningful conversations.

How This Book Uses the Word "Confluent"

Throughout this book, you'll notice the term *Confluent Speaker* being used frequently. That's because it encapsulates the journey we're embarking on together.

1. **A Framework for Growth**: The MKPF framework—Mindset, Knowledge, Practice, and Feedback—is designed to help you become a Confluent Speaker. Each chapter will break down how these elements contribute to building both your confidence and fluency.

2. **An Identity**: Being a Confluent Speaker isn't just about speaking English; it's about adopting a new identity. It's about becoming someone who communicates with purpose, clarity, and assurance in any situation.

3. **A Community**: This book isn't just a guide; it's an invitation to join a growing community of Confluent Speakers. Together, we're redefining what it means to speak English confidently and fluently in the real world.

Why I Chose "Confluent" for This Journey

This term reflects the philosophy that learning English is not about achieving a rigid standard but about blending your unique voice, ideas, and personality with the tools of language. Just as two rivers merge to create a stronger, unified flow, confidence and fluency merge to create a speaker who can navigate any conversation.

By the end of this book, my hope is that *Confluent* will not just be a word to you—it will become a part of how you see yourself and your potential. You will not merely *speak* English; you will *own* it with confidence and fluency.

How to Read This Book?

You don't need to follow it step by step. Every learner's journey is different. We all have strengths in some areas and challenges in others. Focus on the chapters that resonate with you the most. Skip the ones that don't feel relevant or exciting right now. Revisit certain chapters as many times as you need—once, twice, or even ten times. Fly through some parts, and take your time with others.

Use this book as your canvas. Take notes. Scribble in the margins. Sketch, paint, or draw if it helps you process the ideas. There are no rules, no pressure to follow any specific reading style, and no deadline to finish. Even if you only read one chapter, apply what you learn, and never open the book again, it will still have fulfilled its purpose.

This book isn't just about reading—it's about action. It's about taking what you need and using it to grow, one small step at a time. Let it inspire you, challenge you, or simply be your guide when you feel stuck. However you choose to engage with it, remember, this book is here for you. It's yours to explore, adapt, and make your own. Your journey starts now.

The MKPF Framework

The 4 Essential Ingredients to Becoming a Confident Speaker

Becoming a Confluent Speaker is like cooking a great dish. You can't just throw in a handful of random ingredients and hope for the best. You need the right combination, the right balance, and the right method to make it work. In the same way, to speak with confidence and fluency, you need to develop a combination of key areas.

I know it feels overwhelming. There's so much to do. So many techniques to learn, new words to practice, rules to follow. The pressure can build up, and it can be tempting to avoid speaking in public altogether. But here's the truth: the overwhelm happens when there's no clear system in place. You might learn five new words today, watch a video tomorrow, read a blog the day after—but you don't really see how any of it fits together. You don't know how one task contributes to your overall growth, so it becomes hard to stay motivated.

Without a system, it's like you're trying to build something without a blueprint. You'll always feel lost. But here's where I come in to help you fight that feeling of being overwhelmed and give you the clarity you need to move forward.

I offer you a framework with **4 Essential Ingredients** that will guide you toward becoming a confident speaker. These are the building blocks that every Confluent Speaker must work on:

1. **Mindset**

2. **Knowledge**

3. **Practice**

4. **Feedback**

1. Mindset: The Foundation of Everything

Mindset is the starting point. Without the right mindset, you won't be able to progress. If you think you're not good enough, you'll hold yourself back from even trying. If you think learning English is a destination, you'll give up when you encounter setbacks. But when you understand that fluency is a journey, and you are already on that path, everything changes.

Mindset is about believing that you can do it. It's about knowing that, like anyone else, you have the ability to improve. It's about shifting your perspective from "I can't do this" to "I'm learning, and I'm getting better." You'll face challenges, but with the right mindset, you'll approach them as opportunities to grow, not obstacles to avoid.

2. Knowledge: Filling the Gaps

Knowledge is the next essential ingredient. You need to build a solid foundation of language — vocabulary, grammar, pronunciation — but that's not all. You also need knowledge of the world. You need to understand the context in which you speak. This is why reading books, staying updated, and engaging in conversations is so important. They expose you to different expressions, idioms, and ways of thinking.

But here's where many people go wrong: they focus too much on book knowledge or rules and forget that language is meant to be used in real-life situations. You need knowledge, but it has to be practical and relevant to the conversations you want to have.

3. Practice: Turning Knowledge into Action

Knowledge alone won't make you fluent. You need to practice — consistently and often. Fluency is built by speaking, not just by studying. You have to speak regularly to develop muscle memory, just like any other skill. The more you speak, the more automatic it becomes.

It's like learning how to drive. When you start, you have to consciously think about every move. But after a while, it becomes second nature. Similarly, the more you speak, the more you'll feel in control, and the less effort it will take to express yourself.

But practice doesn't just mean speaking a lot — it also means speaking with purpose. Practice in real, meaningful conversations that challenge you, push you, and give you the opportunity to grow.

4. Feedback: The Mirror You Need

Now, here's where feedback comes in — the ingredient that many people overlook. Feedback is what will make your progress clear. Without feedback, you could keep making the same mistakes over and over without even realizing it.

Think about a doctor diagnosing a patient. The patient might not notice the small symptoms that are causing discomfort, but a doctor can detect them right away. Similarly, you might not realize the small mistakes you're making while speaking, but a coach or mentor can help you identify them.

Feedback gives you the objective perspective you need to improve. It allows you to correct your mistakes and refine your speaking skills. Without it, you'll be blind to your weaknesses, and without knowing where you're going wrong, you won't be able to grow.

Putting It All Together

You see, all four ingredients — mindset, knowledge, practice, and feedback — work together to build your fluency and confidence. You can't skip any one of them and still expect to succeed.

If you have all the knowledge in the world but no practice, you'll panic when you need to speak. If you practice a lot but don't receive feedback, you'll keep making the same mistakes and feel stuck. And if your mindset isn't in the right place, you'll constantly doubt yourself and avoid speaking altogether.

But when you combine all four ingredients and work on them consistently, you will unlock your true potential as a Confluent Speaker.

So, stop looking for shortcuts. Stop focusing on just one area and neglecting the others. Embrace the system, and trust that with time, effort, and the right guidance, you will become a fluent, confident speaker.

SECTION 1

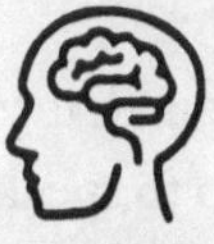

Mindset

Mindset:
The Foundation of Your Confluent Journey

The truth is, the biggest barrier to speaking confidently isn't always a lack of knowledge—it's a lack of the right mindset.

Over the years, I've worked with countless individuals who had the knowledge—good grammar, vocabulary, even excellent pronunciation. But they still weren't speaking confidently. And I've seen that it's never about knowing more or practicing more techniques. It's always about *how* they saw themselves as speakers. It's about their mindset.

If your mind tells you that you're not good enough, you'll never take the leap to speak. If you doubt your own abilities, your words will falter before they leave your lips. It doesn't matter how much you know—your mind controls your actions. And this is the foundation where many language learners struggle, even after years of study.

I've witnessed this firsthand in my sessions with students. They know the rules, they know the vocabulary, but the moment they need to speak—whether it's in front of a crowd, in a meeting, or in a casual conversation—they freeze. They hesitate. They hold themselves back. They don't speak because they're afraid of making mistakes, of being judged, of sounding "wrong." These fears come from a deeper belief that they aren't capable, that they aren't ready.

This is where the work begins.

This section is dedicated to shifting your mindset because that shift is what unlocks everything. Once your mindset changes, everything else becomes possible. It's about transforming the way you see yourself as a speaker, shedding the limiting beliefs, and embracing the courage to speak—even when you feel unsure, unprepared, or nervous.

In the following chapters, we'll dive deep into the key aspects that will shape your mindset. We'll break through the layers of fear and self-doubt that are holding you back from speaking confidently. You'll discover:

1. **How to embrace your current level of fluency** – No more waiting for "perfection." You're already fluent, and it's time to recognize that.

2. **The power of a "growth mindset"** – How seeing language learning as a journey, not a destination, allows you to embrace mistakes and learn from them.

3. **Why you should stop fearing fear** – We'll break down how fear of speaking actually holds you back and how you can shift your relationship with fear.

4. **How to develop your identity as a Confident Speaker** – It's about becoming the type of person who speaks confidently, rather than just someone who knows English.

5. **Becoming an independent learner** – How to step away from the dependence on others for validation and take ownership of your growth.

I've seen time and again how a shift in mindset can transform a learner's journey. And once you unlock this, the entire process of speaking, learning, and growing becomes easier, more natural, and more fulfilling.

Let's break through those barriers together and start your transformation into a Confluent Speaker, one mindset shift at a time.

CHAPTER 1

Speaking By Speaking Philosophy

My father used to say, *"Bolne se bolna aata hai, likhne se likhna aata hai aur padhne se padhna aata hai."*

As a child, I didn't fully understand the depth of this simple yet powerful sentence. But as I grew older, the wisdom behind those words became crystal clear. I still carry this truth with me today, especially as I reflect on my own journey and the countless learners I've worked with.

Take this book, for example. I've wanted to write it for a long time. But it wasn't until I finally started—writing every single day for 120 days—that the first draft was ready. I didn't wait for the "right time," or for a moment when I felt fully prepared. I simply started, and through that consistent effort, it all came together. *I wrote this book by writing this book.*

And this approach, this mindset, can be applied to your own language learning journey. If you want to become a confident, powerful speaker, you need to speak. *You will not become powerful first and speak later. You need to speak first, and the confidence will follow.* Confidence isn't something you wait for; it's something that builds as you act, step by step.

Stop fooling yourself into thinking that consuming content—watching videos or reading tips on the internet—is the real progress. While these things are helpful, they won't give you the confidence you're seeking. *The real progress comes from taking speaking opportunities*—even when you're scared. Every time you speak to someone in English, even if you're afraid, every time you get up on stage trembling, every time you try out a new word, your confidence will grow.

Bolne se bolna aata hai.

Of course, reading is valuable—it will make you a better reader. But becoming a better speaker requires something more. *A better speaker is made by speaking.* Just like Sachin Tendulkar became the cricket legend he is by stepping onto the field, not by reading about cricket, or like Nawazuddin Siddiqui's acting mastery developed by taking on roles in dramas and movies, not by just listening to acting tips. *Do what you want to learn, rather than learning about what you want to do.*

In the same way, you will become a Confident Speaker only by speaking. This is the foundation. *Mindset* isn't about waiting for the perfect moment to speak, or perfecting every little detail before you take action. It's about embracing the courage to speak, no matter how unsure you feel, because that's how you'll grow.

> *Speak to grow, not to be perfect.*

CHAPTER 2

It's Inside

If you're at least a graduate, there's a strong chance that you already have a good foundation in English. We live in an era where we consume a massive amount of English content daily—whether it's Hollywood movies, global politics, US YouTubers, or British travelers. We're surrounded by this content, and it's not just entertainment. It's a constant source of language exposure.

Living in a digital world gives us access to English practice even if we haven't moved to an English-speaking country. With platforms like YouTube and social media, we're already part of an English-speaking circle, learning without even realizing it. This vast exposure to English helps us without us having to actively "study" it, making it easier to enhance our skills, step by step.

But here's the catch: *to truly improve*, you need to remove the excess "old oil" in your system before you can make room for the new. Just like when you service your car or bike and change the engine oil, you remove the old oil first, knowing that the old residue can spoil the fresh one. Similarly, in language learning, you need to clear away any mental blocks, limiting beliefs, or outdated habits you might be holding onto before you can effectively move forward.

Your English potential is already within you. The key is in bringing it out and giving it space to grow.

This is the foundation of true language growth—getting comfortable with what you already know and practicing it in real-life situations. The process isn't about learning new things only; it's about unlocking the knowledge you already possess and using it. By practicing consistently, speaking with confidence, and allowing yourself to make mistakes, you'll naturally see progress, bit by bit, as your existing knowledge transforms into active, fluent speech.

> *Fluency isn't about words; it's about connection.*

CHAPTER 3

Identity Shift

When you start following the method of learning through speaking, something powerful begins to happen—you undergo an *identity shift*. This shift doesn't need to be a dramatic moment; it can happen at any point in this journey. But once your identity transitions from a learner to a speaker, your entire world and perception will change.

You will no longer see yourself as someone who is *learning* English. You'll start to see yourself as a speaker who is continuously improving. This shift isn't just about adding more vocabulary or perfecting grammar—it's about shifting how you view yourself and your relationship with the language.

Think about it: instead of saying, "I'm not an English speaker," start saying, "I am a speaker who is getting better every day." This simple change in perspective is where your growth begins. It's the foundation of the mindset shift you need to truly progress.

Changing your mindset is crucial. It's the catalyst for change in your entire journey. When you shift your identity, everything else follows suit.

Imagine this: two people are stuck in the same traffic jam. One person is frustrated, fidgeting in their seat, their mind racing with irritation, while the other person remains calm, listening to music or enjoying a podcast, completely at ease. Both are facing the same traffic, the same situation, yet their reactions are entirely different. Why? Because their identity and mindset are different. One person sees themselves as someone who *can't stand* delays, while the other sees the situation as just part of the journey.

This is the power of identity. Changing your mindset towards speaking English can have the same transformative effect. When you adopt the mindset of a speaker, your world opens up. Every challenge, every mistake, becomes a stepping stone rather than an obstacle.

Unfortunately, many people aren't even aware of the identity they're carrying with them. They may walk around thinking they're just "bad at English," "shy," or "not good enough" without realizing that these thoughts are what hold them back. It's time to take control of your own narrative.

Shift from being a *learner* to being a *speaker*. Embrace the process, celebrate the progress, and watch how your world shifts as you step into the role you were always meant to play.

> *The more you fail, the faster you learn.*

CHAPTER 4

Becoming An Independent Learner

You cannot learn English—or any language—by relying on short-term courses. These courses are there to provide extra support, but ultimately, they cannot do the work for you. Your coach cannot speak for you. The best they can do is help you find the courage and confidence to speak up. The real work, the real progress, comes from you.

Think of it this way: if you have all the best spices and ingredients but no one to cook the meal, what use are they? The courses, books, and resources are your ingredients. But you, *you* are the one who has to put them to use. It's about becoming an independent learner, taking responsibility for your own growth and learning journey.

You can take courses, read books, and learn from various sources—that's the right approach. But here's the trap: many people think that a course will magically solve their problem or a book will provide the missing piece of their language-learning puzzle. That's a misconception. It doesn't work like that. There is no quick fix, no shortcut. You will need to consistently upgrade your language skills over many years. And that's perfectly okay.

Why is that? Because language learning is a lifelong journey. There are different levels, like the CEFR (Common European Framework of Reference for Languages) levels, and your goals depend on your current stage in life. Just as you don't teach a 3rd-grade student the same thing as a 10th-grade student (except for rare exceptions), you can't expect the same resources to work for everyone at every level. For example, a conversation club may not be helpful if you're a beginner, but it can work wonders if you're an intermediate learner lacking confidence. Similarly, a basic grammar course won't do much for an advanced learner, but it can help someone who is just getting started. Different challenges require different solutions.

I want you to adopt a more expansive attitude towards language learning. Think of it like parenting. As a parent, you need to adjust your approach depending on your child's age and developmental stage. You can't teach a 5-year-old to write an essay, nor would you give a teenager a picture book and expect them to learn the same way. Similarly, your approach to language learning should be dynamic and adjusted to where you currently are.

When you become an independent learner, you take ownership of your journey. You don't wait for the perfect course or the right book; you actively seek out the resources that suit your needs, and you use them in a way that fits your current stage. That's when the real progress begins.

Now, to help you navigate your progress, **assessments** are key. Many learners struggle because they don't know where they stand or how far they've come. Knowing your current level—both overall and in specific areas—is crucial for growth.

Start with the **CEFR levels**, which categorize your language proficiency into six levels:

- **A1 (Beginner)**: Basic communication skills in simple situations.

- **A2 (Elementary)**: Able to understand and use familiar everyday expressions.

- **B1 (Intermediate)**: Can deal with most situations in daily life and express opinions.

- **B2 (Upper Intermediate)**: Can produce clear, detailed text on complex subjects.

- **C1 (Advanced)**: Can use language fluently and flexibly in social, academic, and professional settings.

- **C2 (Proficient)**: Mastery of the language, with full fluency and accuracy.

You can assess your **overall language level** by taking online placement tests from trusted platforms. These tests will give you an idea of where you stand in terms of grammar, vocabulary, listening, reading, writing, and speaking. Once you know your CEFR level, you'll have a clearer understanding of where to focus your efforts.

But don't stop at just overall language assessments. The beauty of becoming an independent learner is that you can evaluate **specific areas** of your language skills. If you want to improve your **reading** skills, look for **reading comprehension tests**. If **grammar** is an area you struggle with, there are countless grammar quizzes available online that will pinpoint where you need more focus. **Listening skills**? Assess them by listening to podcasts or watching videos in English and taking tests on the material. You can even take specific **placement tests** for different English skills, which allow you to target areas that are holding you back.

By regularly assessing yourself, you can identify areas that need improvement and track your progress. This helps you stay motivated because you can see tangible growth, even if it's small steps. This process will guide your learning and keep you on the right track, ensuring that you're not just guessing where you are but actively knowing what to work on next.

So, assess yourself regularly, set new goals based on the results, and adjust your learning resources accordingly. The more precise and tailored your approach, the quicker you'll move towards fluency. The journey may seem long, but with these assessments as your compass, you'll keep heading in the right direction.

> *Confidence starts when you step into discomfort.*

CHAPTER 5

Don't Fear Fear - Understand It

Why do you feel low on confidence? It's simple: Fear. At the core of every hesitation to speak up, every reluctance to try, lies fear. The fear of speaking English, the fear of standing out, the fear of making mistakes, and most commonly, the fear of looking foolish. You may also fear others' judgment—worrying that people will laugh at you or criticize your efforts. And yet, the truth is that those fears are often exaggerated, overblown by your own mind.

At the heart of it all, your fear is about **reputation**. You are worried about how your communication skills, or lack thereof, will affect your image. You don't want to be judged, ridiculed, or seen as less than perfect. So, you avoid speaking English. You tell yourself, "I will speak only when I'm perfect. Only when I make no mistakes." But guess what? That day will never come. Perfection is a myth. The only way to get better is through practice, through speaking—mistakes and all.

You may tell yourself that you can't speak because you're not "ready." But the truth is, you'll never feel "ready" until you take that first step. Fear will always find an excuse, always provide a reason for why you shouldn't do something. But if you allow it to control you, if you keep avoiding speaking, your fear will **never** go away. You have to face your fears head-on.

Let me explain it like this: Imagine a street dog chasing you. If you run away, it will chase you faster, right? The fear only intensifies the more you try to escape. But if you stand still, if you turn around and face that dog, most of the time, it will stop. It will realize you're not running away, and it will lose interest. The same applies to fear. The more you run from it, the stronger it gets. But when you confront it—when you speak up in English despite the fear—it starts to lose its power over you.

Facing your fears doesn't mean they vanish instantly. No, it takes time. It won't go away by simply watching motivational videos or reading inspiring books. It goes away through action. Through doing. By stepping out of your comfort zone and speaking English even when you're not perfect.

The fear of making mistakes or sounding foolish will always be there—because we all have it. But what sets apart confident speakers is their ability to **not let that fear control them**. They speak anyway. They learn through mistakes. They see errors as stepping stones, not failures.

I want you to understand that fear is not something to run from. Fear is not the enemy. Fear is your mind telling you that you're about to step into a new, unfamiliar territory. And that's exactly where growth happens. Fear means you're growing. Fear means you're on the verge of something important.

So, instead of avoiding it, I encourage you to face it. Speak up. Make mistakes. Laugh at yourself if you need to. And then try again. Your fear is only holding you back because you've given it control. But the moment you take action, the moment you speak despite the fear, you take that control back.

In the end, fear is a sign. A sign that you're challenging yourself, that you're stepping into new territory. And remember—no one gets better without a little discomfort. So, embrace that discomfort. Understand your fear, and **face it boldly**. Only then will you truly start to grow as a speaker.

Don't let fear stop you. **Stand firm.**

To speak fluently, first speak fearlessly.

CHAPTER 6

How to See Courses

In the last chapter, we talked about fear—the fear of speaking, making mistakes, and standing out. Now, let's dive deeper into what stops many people from moving forward: the false belief that a course or coaching program will be the magic key to becoming a powerful speaker overnight.

This is where many learners get stuck. They think that just one course or coaching session will solve all their problems. But here's the thing: language learning is not a one-time fix. It's a lifelong journey. There's no course that will make you fluent in 30 days. No magic program that will instantly transform you into a confident speaker.

Many people reach out to me, telling me they want to become a more powerful speaker. Some say they have one month to prepare for an interview. Others give even more extreme deadlines, like the person who called me and said, "Sir, mujhe English sikhna hai, parso mera interview hai!" (Sir, I need to learn English, my interview is the day after tomorrow!).

Don't be that person

You can't rush fluency or expect a quick fix. But you can use courses and coaching programs to accelerate your progress. Think of them like a turbo boost for your language journey. Instead of relying on them to do all the work, see them as tools that can speed up your growth.

Just like fear won't go away without action, language learning won't progress without consistent effort. However, the right course at the right time can provide you with a structured, focused path forward.

What to Do Instead?

Instead of seeing a course as your only solution to becoming fluent, approach it as an opportunity to level up. Language learning is ongoing, but a course can give you the boost you need at any stage. Whether you're a beginner or an intermediate speaker, there's always room for improvement—and that's where courses come in.

Here's how to think about it:

1. **Use courses as speed-ups**. They're meant to help you move faster towards your language goals. But, just like we talked about in the previous chapter, facing your fear and speaking is the core of your progress. Courses can accelerate that, but they aren't substitutes for real, on-the-go practice.

2. **Target specific areas of improvement**. Is your grammar holding you back? Do you need help with pronunciation or vocabulary? Instead of taking a generic course that promises to solve everything, focus on **specific areas**. For instance, if you're

struggling with a few grammar topics, find a course or program that focuses just on those. This targeted approach will make your language learning more efficient.

3. **View courses as stepping stones**. Once your identity shifts from learner to speaker, courses will no longer be the solution to your fluency. They will become the **tools that take you to the next level**. Just like working with a coach or mentor is meant to challenge you, courses should be used to sharpen your skills.

Remember

Just as fear is something you need to confront to grow, you need to understand that courses aren't the end of the journey, but rather a part of the process. They won't make you fluent overnight, but they can push you closer to your goals faster. Embrace them as tools, not crutches.

Becoming an independent learner means you won't rely on courses to solve everything for you. But using them strategically can accelerate your journey. Just as facing your fears builds confidence, using the right resources wisely will build your fluency.

Remember, the key is in action—and courses are just a way to ensure that action takes you further, faster.

> *Mistakes are the footprints to fluency.*

CHAPTER 7

Your Language is Always Growing

Your Language is Always Growing

As we transition from the last chapter, where we discussed how courses and coaching can accelerate your progress, let's explore a vital truth: your language is always growing—even when you don't realize it.

Many people think they have wasted time if they haven't taken formal classes or followed a rigid learning path. But that's far from the truth. Language growth happens everywhere—whether you realize it or not. It's happening all the time, in ways both big and small, and it's up to you to recognize it as progress.

Consider this: when you look back at your English skills from two years ago, how much have they grown? You might not see it in the moment, but just by being immersed in English, even passively, your brain is constantly absorbing new words, phrases, and structures. This is all a part of your ongoing language development.

In a world that's super connected and accessible, language learning has no boundaries. And for many of us, especially in places like India, we've already been exposed to a lot of English—through movies, social media, news, and even casual conversations. We may think we're not actively learning or improving, but every single time you hear, read, or watch something in English, your language is evolving.

You may not always see it consciously, but subconsciously, your brain is picking up new vocabulary, grammar structures, and ways of speaking.

For instance, in the local trains of Mumbai, I learned a new word—*alighting*—which means "getting off the train," just from hearing it in the announcements: *"Please mind the gap between the footboard and the platform while alighting from the train."* You may have learned words like this, too, without even realizing it. These small moments add up, making your language richer and more fluid over time.

Be in the Language Atmosphere

The key here is immersion. Even if you aren't actively studying English every day, if you surround yourself with it, your language will grow. Whether it's reading articles, watching videos, listening to interviews, or simply interacting with people who speak English, each exposure counts.

The same principle applies to things like social media, news, books, or conversations with friends. Every time you engage with English, even in small doses, you feed your language plant. It's like watering a plant: the more you engage, the more it thrives.

In fact, you might even notice that you start to speak like your favorite celebrities. The more you watch interviews or listen to them, you might find that their way of speaking influences yours. You start to pronounce words in a similar way or use certain pauses like they do. This is your language absorbing influences from the world around you, much like a sponge soaking up water. It happens naturally—without effort, but always growing.

From Passive Learning to Active Growth

This continuous, passive exposure to English doesn't just make you more familiar with the language; it actually shapes the way you speak. It's like having a conversation with the world itself, where each word and phrase you come across adds to your personal vocabulary and style.

Just as courses and coaching can accelerate your learning, this daily exposure acts as an organic growth system for your language skills. It's not always about formal study or structured lessons—it's about creating a lifestyle of language interaction.

The trick is to stay aware of this growth. Even when you're not consciously learning, your language is evolving. Embrace it. Whether you're hearing words in a movie, reading a caption on Instagram, or listening to a podcast, every single moment is contributing to your fluency.

So, don't underestimate the power of the environment you create around your language learning. Your exposure to English—through everyday experiences, media, and interactions—can become a lifelong investment in your growth as a fluent, confident speaker.

You are already learning. Your language is already growing. The question is, are you recognizing it?

> *Listening first, speaking second—that's fluency.*

CHAPTER 8

A Confident Speaker

What's Confidence?

As we dive deeper into the journey of becoming a confident and fluent speaker, it's important to first ask yourself: What is confidence?

A powerful speaker is someone who embraces the fact that they don't know everything. And guess what? That's their power. They understand that learning and growth are never-ending processes. They accept that they won't be perfect today, tomorrow, or ever—and that's completely okay. A confident speaker knows that their speaking journey is always evolving, and they keep moving forward, no matter what.

Confidence isn't about being perfect. It's not about speaking flawlessly or having every word ready. It's about being okay with imperfection and knowing that you are enough—right here, right now. It's about speaking, even when you're scared.

You see, many times, I find myself motivating others while going through some of the most difficult challenges in my own life. But, just like you, I choose to speak anyway. A confident speaker doesn't let life's challenges control their performance. No matter the personal struggles or fears, they show up and do what they do best: they speak.

Speaking Despite Fear and Doubt

A confident speaker speaks even when they're scared. They speak even when they're unprepared. They speak even when they're not sure—and yes, even when they're not grammatically perfect. What sets them apart isn't their flawless delivery; it's the decision to speak regardless of their doubts, fears, or insecurities.

It's easy to believe that only those who are perfectly composed or absolutely certain of their words can be confident. But in reality, true confidence comes from acknowledging your fears and moving forward anyway. It's okay to feel fear, doubt, and uncertainty—what matters is what you do with those feelings. You don't let them paralyze you. You acknowledge them, and you keep speaking.

The Power of Small Speaking Opportunities

Confidence is not built overnight. It's a day-by-day growth. Every time you choose to speak, you are increasing your confidence, no matter how small the opportunity might seem. Think about the moments you've passed up—those chances where you held back because you were unsure or afraid. Imagine if you had taken just 10 more chances to speak in those situations. Where would your confidence be today?

It's the small wins that matter. One meeting where you speak up, one presentation where you share your thoughts—those are the moments that gradually increase your confidence. Don't underestimate them. Each time you step up, even with a little fear, you are growing your speaking muscle.

You're building the foundation for the speaker you want to become. Consistency is key. Every day you speak, even in imperfect circumstances, is one step closer to where you want to be. So, when you face an opportunity today, don't avoid it. Embrace it.

Your confidence doesn't depend on perfection; it depends on your willingness to keep going, even when it's tough. The more you speak, the more confident you'll become.

> *Don't aim for accuracy—aim for action.*

CHAPTER 9

Self-Sabotage

How You Kill Your Confidence

As we've discussed in the previous chapter, confidence is a journey. It's about showing up, even when you're scared. It's about speaking even when you're unsure, and embracing the process of growth. But what happens when you're your own worst enemy? When, despite your best efforts, you find yourself holding back? That's where self-sabotage creeps in.

Self-sabotage is one of the biggest killers of confidence. We all have it. You, me, and everyone else. Some of us have it in small doses, while others may struggle with it more. But the reality is, we all have those tendencies, habits, people, and commitments in life that we know are holding us back. Yet, for some reason, we continue to feed them, even when we know they are detrimental to our growth.

We sabotage ourselves in subtle ways. We tell ourselves, "I can't speak confidently," and before we know it, that belief becomes our reality. This belief is the root of your struggle. It's the reason why so many learners, even when they're already at an intermediate level, continue to say they can't speak English. And that's exactly why they can't.

I've met countless learners who come to me for help, already at a B1 or B2 level of English. And what do they say? "I can't speak English." I don't buy that. When I start speaking to them in English, they're often surprised to realize they're not as bad as they thought. The truth is, they've been feeding themselves the story that they can't communicate. And as long as they believe that, they continue to hold themselves back.

In his book *Turning Pro*, Steven Pressfield describes how, in wars, some soldiers would shoot their own legs to avoid the real battle. It's a bizarre, extreme example, but it's powerful. These soldiers would literally sabotage their own efforts to avoid facing the challenges ahead. This sounds extreme, but we do this in our own way. Instead of showing up to speak and face our fears, we shoot ourselves in the foot. We tell ourselves, "I can't do this," and we back away from the very opportunities that could help us grow. We sabotage ourselves, again and again, because we're afraid of failing or not being perfect.

How Self-Sabotage Kills Your Confidence

When you continuously tell yourself that you can't do something, you begin to believe it. Every time you avoid speaking, every time you second-guess yourself, you reinforce the idea that you're not good enough, that you're not confident enough. This creates a negative feedback loop. The more you avoid speaking, the less confident you become. The less confident you feel, the more you avoid speaking. It's a vicious cycle.

But here's the thing: You are already capable. Just like those learners who were surprised to find that their English was not as bad as they thought, you're probably much more capable than you give yourself credit for. Your potential is locked away in the belief that you're not enough. Your fear of failure is the real barrier.

So, how do you break this cycle? Recognize the self-sabotage. Catch yourself when you're telling yourself, "I can't speak" or "I'm not good enough." Then, take the next step: Speak anyway. Even if you feel scared, even if you're not prepared, speak. Every time you break through that fear, your confidence will grow. Every small speaking opportunity you take is a victory over self-sabotage.

Don't shoot your own leg to avoid the battle. Face it, and speak anyway. That's how you build true confidence.

The Real Power Is In Your Mindset

Remember, you are the cause and the cure of your struggles. "Dard-e-dil ki wajah bhi tum, shifa bhi tum"— you are the reason you're struggling, but you are also the solution. You have the power to change the narrative. Stop believing in the self-sabotage. Stop shooting yourself in the foot. It's time to show up for yourself. Speak up, take action, and watch your confidence grow with every step.

You are capable of far more than you realize. It's time to stop holding yourself back. It's time to face the challenge or what Steven Pressfield would say **"It's time to turn pro"**.

(Footnote: *Shifa* is an Urdu word meaning "healing" or "cure," often used metaphorically to refer to the solution or remedy for a problem.)

> *Less grammar, more conversation.*

CHAPTER 10

So What? - You're Not a Celebrity

Let's face it. A lot of us hold back from speaking, from making mistakes, from growing, because we're terrified of what others might think. *What if people laugh at me? What if I forget my lines? What if my grammar is wrong? What if I mispronounce something?*

So what?

Seriously. *So what?*

You're not a celebrity. The world will not come to a screeching halt just because you mispronounced a word or made a grammatical error. No one will write a headline about your mistake tomorrow. You won't lose your job, and you definitely won't be thrown in jail for not speaking perfectly.

Think about the price you're paying. How much time are you wasting? How many years will you let pass just because you're so wrapped up in what others might think of your English?

Now, it's time to ask yourself—*When will you start thinking about yourself and your growth?* How many more opportunities will you let slip by simply because you're so concerned about your image?

YOU ARE NOT A CELEBRITY—and that's a good thing. You don't need to live up to some unreal standard. Making mistakes isn't a tragedy. In fact, it's a stepping stone to fluency and confidence.

Next time you feel scared, ask yourself: *So what if I make a mistake?* And the answer will be: *So nothing.*

Nothing at all. Because no one is going to care as much as you think they will. Most people have much bigger things to worry about in their lives than whether your grammar was perfect. And if they do judge you for your mistakes? Well, they're called English teachers. And even they make mistakes too.

Your fears are irrational. They're just holding you back from becoming the speaker you're meant to be. You've got to look at them without emotion, without drama. When you do, you'll realize how small and insignificant those fears truly are.

So, my friend, it's time to speak. Speak with mistakes. Speak with errors. Speak with courage. And remember— if you never try, you'll never know. Without falling, you can't grow. Without practice, you can't get better.

So what if you make a mistake? You'll learn, you'll grow, and you'll become the confident, fluent speaker you've always wanted to be. Keep going. Speak. And *so what?* Nothing is stopping you.

> *To be fluent, you must be okay with being wrong.*

CHAPTER 11

The Price and the Prize

Often, we don't take action on the things we know we should be doing because we don't truly understand the price we are paying by not doing them. It's like mindlessly scrolling through social media—you don't realize the cost until you reflect on the time wasted.

The same applies to language learning. You know you need to improve your English, but you don't always put in the effort. You know the prize—better communication skills, more opportunities, growth in your career—but you're not fully aware of the price of inaction.

The Prize is clear: if you improve your communication skills, you will gain access to better opportunities. Powerful speakers stand out and get noticed. In all my years of coaching, I can tell you that no one has ever asked me about my degree before joining my courses. In fact, most of my students still don't know my qualifications—and they don't care. What they value is my confidence, my approach, and my ability to help them communicate effectively. A confident speaker earns trust without needing to prove anything.

But instead of only focusing on the rewards, it's important to recognize **the price** of inaction. Ask yourself, *What is it costing me not to act?*

Here's what it costs:

1. **Missed Opportunities**: If I'm not a confident speaker, I'm already missing out on opportunities that could have been mine.

2. **Strained Relationships**: Without confidence in speaking, I'm already straining my relationships and missing chances to connect.

3. **Stagnant Career**: If I lack confidence, my career growth is slowing down. Promotions and raises are passing me by.

4. **Loss of Respect**: When I'm not confident, I'm losing people's attention and respect.

5. **Self-Doubt**: If I doubt myself when speaking, I'm already feeling worse about myself.

6. **Stress**: When I'm afraid to speak up, I'm already dealing with the stress of missed opportunities.

7. **Perception of Incompetence**: Others might see me as less capable if I don't speak with confidence.

8. **Feeling Stuck**: If I don't speak up, I'm watching others move forward while I stay stuck.

9. **Overall Limitation**: The cost of not speaking confidently is holding me back in every aspect of life.

But, as with anything, there's another side to this—the prize for speaking confidently is just as clear:

1. **Seizing Opportunities**: If I become a confident speaker, I'll be able to seize opportunities that were once out of reach.

2. **Stronger Relationships**: Confidence in speaking will help me build stronger, more genuine connections.

3. **Career Advancement**: Becoming a confident speaker will open doors to career growth, new opportunities, and promotions.

4. **Commanding Respect**: Confidence allows my words to carry weight, earning me respect and attention.

5. **Self-Esteem**: As a confident speaker, I'll bolster my self-esteem and feel better about myself.

6. **Stress-Free Communication**: Speaking with confidence will ease my stress, helping me navigate challenges smoothly.

7. **Enhanced Perception**: Others will perceive me as capable, competent, and credible.

8. **Leadership**: Confidence in speaking will position me as a leader, enabling me to inspire and lead others.

9. **Unlocking Potential**: By embracing confidence, I'll unlock my full potential, impacting my life positively in every way.

The price is high. But the prize? It's worth it. The choice is in your hands—will you pay the price, or will you step into the prize that's waiting for you? The cost of not acting today is too high. Let your actions today shape the future you deserve tomorrow.

Now that we've understood the heavy price of self-sabotage and the priceless reward of confidence, the choice is clear. It's in your hands to decide whether you'll continue to hold yourself back or step forward into the power of self-belief.

With the right mindset now in place, we're ready to move to the next pillar of the Confluent Speaker Framework—Knowledge. When you have the right mindset, the knowledge you gain will take your speaking skills to a whole new level. Let's explore how to use this knowledge to unlock your full potential and make real progress on your journey to becoming a truly confident, fluent speaker.

> *The less you think, the more you speak.*

SECTION 2

Knowledge

Just like mindset, knowledge is a core pillar of becoming a Confluent Speaker. And here's the thing—knowledge isn't just about language rules. It's about expanding the scope of what you know and how you engage with the world around you. Sure, grammar, vocabulary, pronunciation, and even intonation are essential, but to become truly confident and fluent in English, you must also enrich your understanding of the world.

Think about this: when we talk about Confluent Speakers, we're talking about those who can speak with confidence and fluency, not just in English, but about a range of topics—from technology to global politics, from current events to health trends. To speak with conviction and make an impact, you need to be able to talk about things that matter, things that are happening right now, things that make you an interesting person to converse with. And this kind of knowledge isn't just academic—it's about being engaged with life.

Take, for example, someone like Shah Rukh Khan. He's not just a great English speaker; he's a great conversationalist because he has knowledge beyond language. He knows about the world—what's happening in politics, technology, culture, and human nature. That knowledge allows him to speak with authority, to be relevant, and to connect with people from all walks of life. To become a Confluent Speaker, you need to understand that knowledge of the world—your curiosity, your ability to connect the dots, and your interest in everything around you—gives you the confidence to speak freely.

Knowledge fuels your fluency. You can't be fluent in speaking about something if you don't have any knowledge about it. But when you actively engage with different fields—be it artificial intelligence, global affairs, science, or art—you'll have more to talk about, more to connect with, and more to share in your conversations. The more you know, the more confident you will feel, and the more fluent you will become in your ability to express yourself on any subject.

So, how do you build this knowledge? It's about staying curious and being engaged. It's about reading, watching, listening, and asking questions. You don't need to be an expert in every field, but being curious about the world will give you enough material to speak confidently.

This section will show you how to broaden your knowledge base, not just to sound smart, but to speak with true confidence. Let's dive into this exciting exploration of knowledge and see how it can fuel your transformation into a Confluent Speaker.

CHAPTER 12

Grammar Knowledge

The Balance Between Perfection and Progress

As we continue our journey to becoming Confluent Speakers, one of the first things I want to address is grammar. Let me be clear: grammar **is** important, but it **is not** the only thing that defines a confident and fluent speaker.

So many language learners get caught up in the pursuit of perfect grammar. They want to avoid mistakes, they fear sounding "wrong," and they believe that every sentence must be flawless. But here's the truth—**perfection is a myth**. The goal isn't to pass a grammar exam or to speak like a grammar textbook. The goal is to communicate effectively and confidently. If you make mistakes along the way, that's okay. In fact, it's a necessary part of the learning process.

Now, don't get me wrong, you do need a strong foundation in grammar to speak clearly and accurately. But what's more important is your ability to use grammar naturally in conversation without overthinking every rule. You need to understand grammar well enough so that you don't have to stop and think about it constantly. You need it to become part of your subconscious, so you can focus on your message and your confidence, not your grammar.

Here's a simple, yet powerful strategy that will help you build your grammar knowledge without getting stuck in perfectionism:

- **Get a grammar book**: It doesn't need to be fancy or overwhelming. Get a basic grammar book that covers the essential rules and structures of English. Keep it with you.

- **Pick 10 topics**: Open the index, choose 10 topics that you find interesting or challenging, and mark them. These topics could range from tenses to sentence structure, articles to prepositions—anything that helps you understand how the language works.

- **Study for 2 days per topic**: Give yourself two days to really understand each topic. Read it, study it, and make sure you grasp the concept. It's not about memorizing rules; it's about understanding the logic behind them.

- **Practice, practice, practice**: The key to embedding grammar into your subconscious is **practice**. Don't just read the rules—**use them**. Write sentences. Start with 10, then 15, then 100. Practice as much as you can. This will help solidify the concept in your mind.

- **Use ChatGPT as your guide**: If you don't understand something, ask ChatGPT to explain it to you. Use it as a resource to clarify doubts, break down complex ideas, and help you practice.

When I was a kid, I used to do this religiously. I'd read a grammar topic, then write hundreds of sentences using that rule. By the time I was done, I wasn't consciously thinking about the grammar anymore—it had become second nature. Just like when you run away from a lion out of instinct, your mind starts doing things without you even thinking about them. That's the subconscious mind at work. The same happens with grammar—once you've practiced enough, the rules will come to you naturally when you need them.

Remember this: Fluency isn't about avoiding mistakes; it's about communicating effectively. So, take the pressure off yourself and focus on progress, not perfection. Learn grammar, understand it, but let go of the need to be perfect. It's all part of the process of becoming a confident, fluent speaker.

In the next chapter, we'll dive deeper into other areas of knowledge that contribute to fluency, but for now, make grammar your solid foundation—because with that, you'll be ready to build on everything else.

> *Fluency is a habit, not a talent.*

CHAPTER 13

Knowledge of the World

Now that we've built the foundation with grammar knowledge, let's talk about something that goes beyond the language itself: knowledge of the world.

As we discussed earlier, grammar and vocabulary are important, but they are just the tools you use to express your ideas. What's equally crucial is having something worth expressing in the first place. You can't just rely on grammar and impressive vocabulary to keep people interested. If you don't have a deep understanding of the world around you, your words might sound hollow—no matter how correct or polished they are.

I've seen it countless times: people who speak English fluently, but their conversations feel flat. They can't hold attention. They're the kind of speakers who get through five minutes and you're already looking for an escape. Ever experienced that? Maybe at a school function where someone, completely out of place, gives a long-winded speech and everyone falls asleep. You may have also seen that one speaker who knows how to captivate the room, a comedian, a magician, or even an artist, who isn't necessarily perfect in grammar but grabs your attention with their insights and knowledge.

What do these two types of speakers have in common? One has knowledge of the world, and the other doesn't. And that's exactly the point I'm making.

People don't just want to hear you speak—they want to know *what* you think. Your opinions, your insights, your perspectives—these are the things that make you interesting. But your opinions don't come from just any place. They come from your knowledge—the things you've learned, the experiences you've had, the books you've read, and the people you've interacted with. Your understanding of the world is what gives you depth as a speaker.

To become a Confluent Speaker, you need to develop solid knowledge—not just the illusion of knowledge. It's not enough to memorize facts or repeat information you heard somewhere. You need to truly understand the world around you and form your own opinions. It's about being curious and open to learning, engaging with new ideas, and reflecting on them. This is what gives you the confidence to speak freely, because you'll always have something meaningful to say.

While you're focusing on grammar and pronunciation, make sure to keep expanding your knowledge of the world. And one of the best, most accessible ways to do this is something we all know is important, but often don't make time for: books.

Books are not just about improving your vocabulary— they are gateways to expanding your mind, exploring new ideas, and understanding different perspectives. Read books about history, science, technology, politics, self-improvement, philosophy—anything that interests you. Read widely, and read often. The more knowledge you gather, the more confident and fluent you will become in any conversation, because you'll always have something valuable to contribute.

The world is full of knowledge waiting for you to discover it. So don't limit your learning to grammar books alone. Broaden your horizons. The more you know about the world, the more you'll have to talk about, and the more confident and fluent you'll become as a speaker.

> *Speak before you're ready—learning comes in the doing.*

CHAPTER 14

Books

Fueling Your Confluent Journey

By now, you're beginning to understand that fluency doesn't come from perfect grammar or memorizing vocabulary. It's about a broader knowledge—knowledge of the world and of the ideas that shape it. And one of the most powerful tools for expanding your knowledge is something we all know about, yet often overlook: books.

Now, you're probably thinking, "I know reading is important, but I just can't get into it." I hear you. Many learners start with the best intentions but end up bored, finding it hard to stay engaged. This is not because reading is boring in itself, but because you're often reading things you're *not* interested in. This is a key point that connects to what we've been discussing: interest drives engagement, and engagement drives learning.

If you don't enjoy what you're reading, it's no wonder you get bored. I'll be honest with you—even I, as an avid reader, find it hard to focus if the material doesn't interest me. I've been reading since childhood, but even now, if a book doesn't resonate with my personal interests, it just doesn't grab my attention. That's why it's crucial to read what **you** enjoy, whether it's about your profession, your hobbies, or even something that's just for fun. If you're a health enthusiast, dive into health blogs. If you're into cars and bikes, explore magazines about them. If food excites you, read food blogs. If you're into fashion, fashion magazines.

What's more, reading something from your field of interest doesn't just expand your knowledge—it builds your confidence. Imagine you're a teacher reading about how technology is reshaping education. Or a musician learning about the lives and methods of famous musicians. You'll start to feel more connected to the world around you and see how you fit into the bigger picture.

And, just for fun, let me throw in a challenge: If you're a doctor, maybe start by reading your own handwriting! You'll be surprised how challenging and enlightening that can be.

The point is, you need to read things you care about. Without genuine interest, reading will never be enjoyable, and it won't help you develop fluency. I've seen this firsthand with my learners. One of my clients who is a fashion merchandiser, used to find reading boring and struggled to focus. I gave her a book about fashion and models, and the next day, she couldn't stop talking about how much she'd read. The power of interest made all the difference.

When you read things you care about, you'll naturally want to keep reading, which will expand your knowledge and vocabulary in a way that feels effortless.

And remember, this is all part of your journey towards becoming a Confluent Speaker—combining confidence and fluency. The more you know, the more you'll be able to share. Your opinions will become sharper, your thoughts more refined, and your conversations richer.

So, don't force yourself to read books just because they're "good for you." Instead, find what truly interests you, and let that ignite your passion for reading. The more you enjoy reading, the more you'll grow—not just as a learner, but as a confident, fluent speaker.

> *It's not about speaking faster; it's about speaking clearer.*

CHAPTER 15

Stories

Stories are absolutely crucial to becoming a Confident + Fluent speaker. Stories aren't just for entertainment— they're powerful. They have the ability to engage, inspire, and explain things in ways that dry facts just can't. Think about it. Whether it's a teacher telling you a lesson or your grandmother telling you a story, stories are what we remember. They help us connect, understand, and make sense of the world around us. And guess what? Every time your friend says, "Tujhe pata hai aaj kya hua?"—they're telling you a story. That's how it starts.

Now, how does this help you on your journey to fluency? When you read stories, you're doing so much more than expanding your vocabulary or learning grammar rules. You're learning how to communicate in a way that gets attention. You're learning to simplify complex things and make them relatable to the person you're talking to.

Think about all the stories you've heard growing up— from your parents, your teachers, or your friends. The best lessons come wrapped in a story. When you tell stories in your conversations, you're not just sharing information. You're making it come alive. You're creating connections and making things easier to understand.

Start building your own collection of stories. Look for short stories online, read Zen stories, or dive into stories from your religious texts. These are full of wisdom and can teach you more than you realize. Keep a notebook, or even just a note app on your phone, where you can jot down stories that resonate with you. Then, read them often.

In my own sessions, when I need to explain something complex, I always tell a story. For example, here's one I share with learners who are worried about language learning and confidence building. It's called **"Burning Your Boats."**

The Story of Burning Your Boats: Back in 1519, a Spanish conquistador named Hernán Cortés landed in Veracruz, Mexico, with a mission to conquer the Aztec Empire. But when his troops arrived, he did something unexpected—he ordered them to burn their ships. Why? So that they had no choice but to move forward. There was no way to go back. Cortés knew that by cutting off their escape route, his soldiers would have no option but to commit fully to the mission. This act sparked determination and resolve in his men.

Now, let's relate this to your language learning. Burning your boats in this context means fully committing to the journey. Just like Cortés' soldiers had no way of returning home, you need to immerse yourself in your target language without relying on your native language as a safety net. You'll make mistakes, sure—but that's how you'll grow. By confronting challenges head-on, you'll become more confident and proficient.

Do you see how a story about a war from the past can connect to your language learning today? That's the magic of stories. They make things easier to understand and more impactful. They're not just a tool for learning—they're a way to make your message stick.

So, start gathering stories. Create your own collection. The more stories you have, the more dynamic and impactful your conversations will be. Stories make you an engaging speaker. They add depth, emotion, and interest to your language. And, as you continue to share them, you'll become even more confident in your ability to connect with others.

> *Language isn't a test; it's a tool for connection.*

CHAPTER 16

Unique Things

Let's talk about something that can instantly make your conversations richer and more engaging: your unique knowledge and experiences.

You might not even realize it, but you already have stories and knowledge that are special to you. They don't need to be extraordinary or something you read in a book. It's about understanding the value of what you already know.

Have you ever stopped to think about the stories from your childhood? Or the experiences you've had from your hometown, village, or travel? These things are unique to you. And when shared in conversation, they create a connection that no textbook knowledge can replicate. Whether it's about the village life you know so well or the international trips you've been on, those stories are what will make your conversations memorable.

The problem is, too many people think they need to learn something new, something *different*, to make their conversations interesting. But here's the truth: Your experiences and knowledge are already unique. You just need to realize how powerful they are.

Society has taught us all to fit in. Take the tech world, for example—Apple launches something new, and suddenly every other company does the same. The same applies to people. You might notice that a lot of people just repeat things they've heard or try to sound like someone else. But here's the catch: You don't need to be anyone but yourself.

Think about it—what do we do when we are trying to sound "good" in a conversation? We start using words or phrases we don't fully understand, trying to mimic what we've seen or heard. It's like a parrot repeating words without knowing the meaning. You don't need to do that. Your conversations don't need to follow a script. They need to follow you.

I'll share something personal to illustrate. I wear the same outfit almost every day—a white shirt, black pants, and trousers. People ask me how I can wear the same thing all the time, but that's how I feel comfortable. That's how I feel powerful and authentic. It's just who I am.

In the same way, language learning doesn't have to be about speaking "properly" or copying someone else's style. Speak the way you speak, not because you think it's what you should sound like, but because it's how you're meant to communicate. Use words that resonate with you, not the ones you think you "should" know. Share your own experiences—they are what will make you stand out.

This connects perfectly with the earlier chapter on stories—think about it. When you share something personal and real, like a travel story or something from your childhood, you're telling a story that only you can tell. Stories are powerful because they bring you into the conversation in a way that no textbook knowledge can. And when you bring your unique experiences to life in a conversation, you create deeper connections.

By embracing your unique knowledge, you become authentic. You start to feel a sense of power and control over your conversations. And remember, this approach connects directly with your mindset (from the first chapter)—the idea that you don't need to be someone else to be effective.

So, the next time you're thinking about a conversation, reflect on your own stories, your experiences, and your unique knowledge. Bring them in! Don't try to be anyone else. Speak your truth, and watch how your conversations become more interesting, impactful, and memorable. This is how you build the confidence to be fluent, just like the power of reading and stories—it all connects.

> *Silence is as powerful as speech—use it wisely.*

CHAPTER 17

Of Course of Your Field

Now that we've talked about how to bring your unique knowledge and experiences into your conversations, it's time to focus on something that's just as essential: mastering your own field.

Of course, all the things we've discussed so far are valuable—stories, unique knowledge, and experiences—they all add richness and depth to your communication. But, here's the thing: none of that matters if you don't have deep, focused knowledge about the field you're in. This is the foundation that will support everything else.

This is something my father used to say, and it's stuck with me: *"I want you to become Mohammed Ali of your field."* He didn't just mean be good at it—he meant master it. Keep learning. Keep improving. Never stop gaining knowledge.

The knowledge of your field is what will give you a competitive edge. It's not enough to just know a little about a lot. If you're a banker, your expertise in finance, economics, and customer relations will set you apart from the rest. The more knowledge you have about your field, the more opportunities open up for you.

If you're in sales, knowing customer psychology and mastering sales techniques can make you a top performer. It's the same for any profession—whether you're a mechanic, a teacher, a lawyer, or a designer. The deeper your knowledge of your field, the better equipped you are to excel.

When you immerse yourself in your field, something magical happens. You start to get that what Robert Greene calls the "fingertip feel"—that deep, intuitive understanding of your work that allows you to think creatively and come up with new ideas. This is when the best solutions come to you. This is when you're able to innovate and push boundaries.

And remember, this doesn't mean you have to become stagnant once you reach a certain level. Mastery isn't a destination—it's an ongoing journey. Just like the way we talked about continuously learning in the previous chapter, the same mindset applies to your field. Never stop learning, never stop growing. Always seek ways to deepen your knowledge and skills. This will not only make you better at your job but will give you the confidence to speak about your field with authority.

So, whether you're dealing with numbers, machines, people, or something else, always be on the lookout for new ways to deepen your understanding. The more knowledge you have, the more power you hold—and that power will shine through in your conversations, your decisions, and your actions.

Now, let's talk about how this connects back to what we discussed before. When you have a deep knowledge of your field, you have something truly valuable to bring to the table—something that no one else can replicate. Your unique experiences and stories will only be enhanced by this expertise. This is how you become authentic and confident, and this is how you set yourself apart in every conversation. Mastering your field gives you that solid foundation to back up all the other tools and insights we've talked about. It's what transforms you from someone who just "knows things" into someone who is truly respected in their field.

The next step? Embrace the continuous journey of learning. Whatever your field is, immerse yourself in it— and watch your opportunities multiply.

> *Confidence is born in the doing, not the knowing.*

CHAPTER 18

Artificial Intelligence & You

We've covered a lot of ground so far, from building your collection of stories, developing your world knowledge to mastering your field. But there's one more tool I want to talk about—**Artificial Intelligence (AI)**.

As an independent learner, you're not always going to be in a classroom or surrounded by a coach or mentor. You'll often find yourself on your own, learning and practicing your language and communication skills. This is where technology, and more specifically AI, can become a powerful ally in your learning journey.

Let's get something straight: **Artificial Intelligence** isn't here to replace human intelligence. It's here to *enhance* it. AI can be a great help in making your learning process more efficient, guiding you, and providing you with valuable resources. But the key is to use AI as a tool—not a crutch.

AI can help you in so many ways.

When it comes to language learning, AI tools can correct your grammar, suggest vocabulary, give you real-time pronunciation feedback, and even provide conversation practice. For example, if you're learning English, you can ask AI to help you with sentence structures, vocabulary usage, or even help you write essays or reports. It's like having a personal assistant available 24/7.

But the magic doesn't stop there. AI can also be an incredible resource for gaining knowledge about the world, your industry, or any field you choose. You can use AI to gather facts, figures, and resources that you need to improve your knowledge in any area. For example, you can ask an AI to explain a complex concept, give you a summary of a book or article, or even generate ideas and creative solutions for a project you're working on.

In your specific field, AI can assist in boosting your knowledge by pulling in information from all corners of the internet, providing insights, and summarizing industry trends. AI can even help you stay updated with the latest research and developments, saving you time and helping you make informed decisions.

However, despite these benefits, AI faces some challenges in India and other regions:

- **Mindset:** There's often hesitation around adopting new technology. People may be intimidated by AI, seeing it as something too advanced or not necessary. But AI is just another tool—an incredibly powerful one that can complement your human capabilities.

- **Lack of Technology:** Not everyone has access to the latest tech that supports AI tools. However, this is slowly changing as technology becomes more affordable and widespread.

- **Lack of Access to Technology:** While some people have access to smartphones and the internet, others may not have reliable connections or devices that support AI tools. This creates a gap in opportunities for some learners.

- **Lack of Training and Guidance:** Many learners aren't sure how to use AI effectively. They might know about its existence but don't know how to harness its full potential.

But these barriers can be overcome. You don't need to know everything about AI to use it effectively. Start small—ask simple questions, use language learning tools, and gradually explore its capabilities. With the right mindset, you can begin integrating AI into your learning and knowledge-gathering process.

Artificial Intelligence is not here to replace your creativity, critical thinking, or human touch. It's here to help you learn faster, become more knowledgeable, and gain deeper insights into your field. If you're a writer, for example, AI can help you brainstorm ideas, refine your sentences, or even edit your drafts. If you're a student, AI can help you practice speaking, improve your writing, or even quiz you on concepts you're studying.

In the end, AI will make you more efficient and capable—but it will never replace the personal effort and passion that you put into learning and mastering your field. The real magic happens when you combine human intelligence with the power of AI. It's about enhancing your natural ability to learn and grow.

So, embrace AI as a tool, not a replacement. Be open to using it in your learning process, whether for language or any other field. Start using it now, and you'll see how it transforms your learning journey—making you more informed, confident, and effective in everything you do.

Keep learning, keep growing, and keep using every tool at your disposal. AI is just one piece of the puzzle, but it's a powerful one.

> *To sound confident, stop worrying about sounding perfect.*

SECTION 3

Practice

In this section, we're going to explore the power of practice and how it plays a crucial role in your journey towards fluency. Knowledge, as we've seen, is essential, but practice is the engine that drives you to real-world communication.

The world is your classroom. Every day, you have countless opportunities to practice English—you just have to find them. Practice doesn't have to be limited to structured lessons or classroom settings. It can happen everywhere: at the mall, in a coffee shop, at a social event, or even while scrolling through your social media feed. Every interaction is an opportunity to speak and practice.

I often like to compare regular practice to something as simple and vital as swimming. If you want to get better at swimming, you don't just study the strokes, you actually get in the water and swim. Similarly, to become fluent in English, you need to speak regularly. There's no substitute for it.

This idea of "creating your own opportunities" is something we'll dive deeper into in the next chapters. You don't need to wait for the perfect moment or for someone to offer you an opportunity. Go out there and create it yourself. Whether it's by engaging with people in your local community, having conversations in English on social media, or practicing through online platforms, the key is to make speaking a regular part of your life.

In the next chapters, we'll look at how you can find opportunities to practice, and how consistent practice will make you more confident and fluent over time. This section is all about empowering you to take control and start practicing because that's the real pathway to fluency.

The Confluent Speaker Framework is not just about acquiring knowledge or theory; it's about applying that knowledge consistently. Through practice, you transform everything you've learned into the confident and fluent communication you're striving for. So, let's dive in and see how practice completes the cycle of learning.

Know It & Do It

We have been growing up using and listening to the phrase "practice makes man perfect". But are We've all heard the phrase, "Practice makes perfect," growing up. But how often do we truly reflect on it? Is it just another catchy phrase we repeat, or do we really embrace and apply its wisdom? Ask yourself: do you understand the true essence of this statement, or is it just something you've heard and passed along like a parrot?

There are so many well-known phrases that we often use without fully realizing their significance. But the power of these words comes when we understand them and apply them consistently. "Practice makes perfect" isn't just about repeating an action over and over—it's about actively engaging with your flaws, accepting them, and growing from them.

Take a moment and think: Are you truly practicing your English, or are you so caught up in your flaws and mistakes that it stops you from speaking? Are you too self-conscious, constantly aware of how you sound, that it actually holds you back from improving?

The key here is action. Know it and then do it. Understanding the principle is just the first step—actual progress happens when you start putting that knowledge into practice. So, the next time you find yourself hesitating, remember that it's your flaws and imperfections that will lead to growth. Every mistake is a step forward, but only if you allow yourself to make those mistakes.

Don't just think about practicing—do it. Speak even when you feel unsure. Only through doing will you build the confidence and fluency you're striving for.

> *Mistakes are your map to success, not your failure.*

CHAPTER 20

Swim Regularly

To become a good swimmer, you need to swim regularly. And to become a better speaker, you need to speak regularly. You already know this. I don't need to tell you, but I'm still reminding you because it's time to wake up and start sharpening your saw. It doesn't take much—a little practice every day, and over time, you'll see amazing results.

Fluency in speaking is like learning how to swim. You can't learn to swim by just reading about it, watching videos, or listening to podcasts. The same goes for speaking—none of these things will make you fluent. They can give you tips, ideas, and strategies, but the real key to fluency is **practice**.

You can only improve by experimenting with what you've learned—and that can only happen through speaking. Just like with swimming, you have to dive in. You must speak regularly. You need to swim every day in the sea of fluency.

At first, it may feel awkward, like dipping your toes into the water. But slowly, you'll grow comfortable. What once felt like a pond will soon feel like a lake, and then a river, and eventually, an ocean. Your confidence and fluency will expand as you swim more often in the language waters.

It's simple: Speak regularly, practice consistently, and over time, you'll see how far you can go. It's all about making the language a part of your daily flow.

> *Fluency isn't about knowing everything; it's about using what you know.*

CHAPTER 21

Speak Aloud

Let's talk about something super simple but powerful: speaking aloud. Seriously, half of your confidence issues while speaking can be solved if you just speak loud enough. Voice is a major part of how we convey confidence, and trust me, your voice can make or break how your message comes across.

Take a moment and think about it: How many times have you been in a conversation or a meeting and someone is speaking so quietly, you have to strain to hear them? It's uncomfortable, right? Now, compare that to someone who speaks with clarity and volume, like *Bapuji* in *Tarak Mehta ka Ulta Chashma*. You know that feeling when he talks and his voice has authority? That's what you want to aim for. No one takes the guy mumbling like *Daya Bhabhi* seriously. I'm sure you've seen how her murmuring doesn't really command respect or attention.

Now, think about it—*Bapuji* doesn't need to scream or shout, but he speaks clearly and with authority. The way he carries himself and the way his voice fills the room makes him stand out in the group. That's the kind of presence we're aiming for in our speaking. Speak aloud, speak clearly, and speak with confidence. The people around you will notice it.

When you speak loud enough, it shows you're comfortable in your own skin. It shows you believe in what you're saying. And just like with the Confluent Speaker Framework, your voice is an important tool that can build your confidence and fluency. Start practicing at home, in front of the mirror, or even while reading out loud—get used to hearing your own voice and getting comfortable with it.

So, let's not be the *Daya Bhabhi* of conversations. Be the *Bapuji*. Speak loud, speak clear, and let your confidence shine through.

> *The best speakers are the best listeners.*

CHAPTER 22

Create Opportunities

Confluent speakers don't wait for opportunities to come to them—they create their own. You can't sit back and hope that the perfect chance to speak will land in your lap. You have to actively seek out and create opportunities for yourself.

Take initiative. Go to your coaching class and ask to speak to your juniors. Offer to help them with what you've learned. Not only will this boost your confidence, but it will also position you as someone who takes action and isn't afraid to step up.

At work, don't wait for someone else to offer you a chance. Approach your HR department and find ways to host office programs or lead meetings. Your HR will appreciate the initiative, and you'll get noticed. More importantly, this could open doors to better opportunities in the future. If your seniors see you performing confidently on stage, you will automatically stand out among your colleagues.

Create moments where you can practice speaking. Whether it's volunteering for presentations, leading discussions, or offering to speak at local events—seek out these chances. The more you put yourself in situations that require speaking, the quicker you'll improve.

Be proactive. The world is full of opportunities—you just need to create them for yourself. By doing this, you're not just waiting for success, you're making it happen.

> *Language doesn't live in textbooks; it lives in conversations.*

CHAPTER 23

Run the Marathon

Becoming fluent in English is not about a quick win. It's not about rushing through a few lessons or cramming vocabulary in a week and expecting to be fluent. It's about taking a long, steady journey where progress happens bit by bit. Fluency in speaking is like running a marathon—it requires patience, persistence, and consistent effort.

Imagine you are a marathon runner. In the beginning, the path might feel tough. You might struggle to keep your pace, and some days, you may feel like quitting. But the key is to not rush. Focus on staying consistent. Every step you take, no matter how small, is progress. There will be moments when you feel exhausted, when you think you can't go any further. But that's when you need to keep pushing. It's not about how fast you run; it's about keeping your momentum, moving forward at your own pace.

Every practice session, every conversation you have, is like a mile in your race. Some days will feel easier than others. Some days you might feel like you've hit a wall. But remember, the marathon isn't won in a few minutes; it's won over time. The more you practice, the more consistent you are, the better your fluency will become.

Just like in a marathon, the reward of fluency comes after sustained effort.

Think of your practice as your training. Just as athletes don't expect to run a marathon without months of preparation, you can't expect fluency to come instantly. But with each passing day, each conversation, and every moment you spend practicing, you are building strength.

So, don't rush the process. Embrace it. Celebrate the small victories along the way. Because just like in a marathon, it's the consistency, the persistence, and the steady effort that will get you to the finish line. Keep running your race, one step at a time.

> *Don't wait for fluency—create it with every word.*

CHAPTER 24

Practice Melts the Ice

When you first start practicing speaking English, your confidence can feel like a solid block of ice—cold, stiff, and hard to move. You might feel nervous, unsure of yourself, and hesitant to speak. It's normal. Everyone goes through that initial stage. But here's the magic—just like ice melts when it's exposed to warmth, your confidence begins to melt with regular practice.

Think about it. The more you practice, the more you start breaking through that barrier of fear and self-doubt. Each time you speak, you're adding warmth to that ice, slowly but surely. At first, it feels tough. Maybe you stumble over your words, or you get self-conscious about making mistakes. But every time you practice, you push that ice a little bit further, and over time, it begins to melt.

The great thing about practice is that it softens those initial blocks of fear, hesitation, and nervousness. It's like chipping away at a giant wall with a small hammer. At first, it seems like nothing is happening. But after a while, you start seeing cracks, and before you know it, the whole wall is crumbling down. Your conversations start to flow more easily, and you begin to feel more comfortable.

As you keep practicing, you become more fluid. You stop overthinking every word, and the ice of your insecurity melts away. You start speaking with confidence, no longer frozen in place by self-doubt. The more you speak, the easier it becomes to express yourself, to connect with others, and to make mistakes without feeling like you're failing.

So, don't worry about that ice you feel when you start practicing. Just keep going. Like melting ice, with every practice session, you'll see that your confidence grows, your words flow more smoothly, and you become more comfortable in your own voice. It's all part of the process.

> *When you forget a word, find another—fluency is resourcefulness.*

CHAPTER 25

Consistency Over Perfection

When it comes to becoming fluent in English, perfection isn't the goal—consistency is. So many people get caught up in trying to speak perfectly, and they end up frustrated or stuck. But here's the truth: perfection is a moving target. The key is to show up regularly and practice, even when it's not perfect.

Think about it: no athlete becomes great by hitting the gym once a month, no musician gets good by playing once in a while. It's the same with language. Your fluency comes from practice, and practice doesn't need to be flawless—it needs to be consistent.

Every time you speak, no matter how small or imperfect the conversation, you are building your skills. You might stumble over words or forget a phrase, but that's progress. You're learning, and learning doesn't happen in one perfect attempt—it happens through repetition, mistakes, and adjustments.

So, instead of waiting for the "perfect moment" to speak or to get everything right, just start. Speak even if you feel unsure. Even if you make mistakes, do it anyway. Consistency will build momentum, and over time, you'll notice that speaking feels more natural, and confidence will follow.

Each small effort compounds, just like compound interest. You won't see the results immediately, but stick with it, and one day, you'll look back and realize how much you've grown. Keep practicing, no matter how imperfect it seems. That's how mastery is built—through consistent, regular practice, not perfection.

> *You speak like you think—think like you speak.*

CHAPTER 26

Push Past Comfort Zones

Fluency isn't found within your comfort zone. It's found when you step outside of it and push yourself into the unknown. If you only practice speaking in familiar situations or with words you already know, you'll stay in the same place. Real growth happens when you stretch your boundaries, challenge yourself, and confront the discomfort of speaking in new ways.

Think about it—when you first learned to ride a bike, it was uncomfortable. Your muscles ached, you wobbled, and you probably fell a few times. But each time you got back up, you were pushing yourself out of your comfort zone and closer to mastery. Language learning is no different.

To improve your speaking skills, you need to embrace the discomfort. This might mean speaking in front of a group, using vocabulary you're not familiar with, or engaging in conversations that feel challenging. It might feel awkward at first, but that's where growth happens.

Maybe you've avoided difficult conversations in English because you're afraid of making mistakes. Or perhaps you stick to certain topics where you feel safe. Now, it's time to push past that comfort. Start by trying new phrases, experimenting with different ways of expressing yourself, and speaking on topics that push your limits.

Remember, every time you challenge yourself, you get closer to becoming the confident, fluent speaker you want to be. So, don't be afraid to step out of your comfort zone. Embrace it. Push yourself further, and you'll see your fluency grow in ways you never imagined. Growth happens in discomfort—so go ahead, push past it.

> *Confidence grows when you're in the conversation, not just watching it.*

CHAPTER 27

Immerse Yourself in the Language

Fluency in speaking comes when you don't just practice speaking occasionally—you live and breathe it. Just like you wouldn't become a good swimmer by dipping in the pool for a few minutes now and then, speaking fluently requires constant practice in real situations. Immersing yourself in speaking English every chance you get is key.

How do you immerse yourself? It's about finding *every opportunity* to speak. Don't wait for the "perfect" moment—create it. You can join conversation clubs, talk with friends who are fluent, or even speak to yourself out loud when you're alone. Think about your day, plan your actions, or talk through a problem—do it all in English. The more you practice, the easier it gets.

When you surround yourself with speaking opportunities, it becomes second nature. You don't need to be in a class or formal setting. For example, you can start small by practicing your English while ordering food at a restaurant, or chatting with a colleague at work. Even casual, everyday conversations add up and help you build your fluency.

You can also turn passive learning into active practice. For example, watch a video or movie in English and repeat the sentences out loud, mimicking the way the characters speak. Record yourself speaking and listen to it to notice areas for improvement. These little moments of speaking, combined throughout the day, lead to bigger breakthroughs.

The more you immerse yourself in speaking practice, the more natural it will become. Soon, you won't even have to think about it—you'll just *speak*. And with regular, immersive practice, you'll find that your confidence and fluency grow quicker than you thought. Speak whenever you can, wherever you can. The language will start to flow naturally, and your comfort with speaking will skyrocket.

> *Speak now, perfect later.*

CHAPTER 28

Practice Under Pressure

After you've immersed yourself in speaking and surrounded yourself with opportunities, it's time to take it a step further—by practicing under pressure. This is where the real growth happens.

When we push ourselves into situations that challenge us, we are forced to think faster, respond more clearly, and be more focused. Whether it's speaking in public, engaging in a difficult conversation, or participating in an interview, the pressure forces you to refine your skills. It's like lifting weights—adding resistance builds strength. Speaking under pressure builds your confidence and sharpens your fluency.

You don't always need to wait for big events to create this pressure. Start small by taking on conversations that make you slightly nervous. Maybe you can speak up more in your group chats, express your opinion in meetings, or participate in an impromptu conversation with someone you don't know well. The key is that these situations push you to think on your feet. Your brain starts working faster, and this kind of real-time thinking improves your fluency and adaptability.

Remember the idea of *immersing yourself in speaking* from the last chapter? Now, bring that immersion into higher-stakes scenarios. Apply what you've learned, but this time with that added pressure. Public speaking, job interviews, or even giving presentations at work or in social situations—these are all opportunities to practice under pressure.

The beauty of practicing under pressure is that you get to see what you really know and where you still need to grow. You'll notice areas where you need more vocabulary or better sentence structure. Most importantly, it helps you stay calm and collected when unexpected moments arise.

And here's the thing: the more you do it, the less pressure you'll feel.

> *The best way to learn is to teach—so talk, even if you're learning.*

CHAPTER 29

The Power of Habit

You've heard it before—*practice makes perfect*. But what truly makes practice powerful is when it becomes a habit. This is where real transformation happens. When speaking regularly becomes something you do without thinking, you've reached a whole new level. It's no longer about forcing yourself to practice; it's just part of who you are. Speaking becomes a natural extension of yourself, like brushing your teeth every morning.

The beauty of habit is that it takes the pressure off. It becomes effortless. Imagine a time when you no longer need to schedule your practice sessions. Speaking English just flows into your day, whether you're talking to someone at work, chatting with friends, or participating in a meeting. You've embedded it into your routine so deeply that you don't even have to think about it.

When you build this kind of consistency, speaking becomes second nature. The nervousness, the hesitation—it fades away. Your brain gets used to the rhythm of the language, and your mouth just follows suit. The more you practice, the more confident you get, and soon, you'll find yourself in conversations without even realizing how much you've improved.

Now that we've explored how powerful practice can be, let's take a moment to reflect. We've covered the importance of *swimming regularly, creating opportunities, practicing under pressure,* and making practice a habit. These are all key to your journey of becoming a more fluent and confident speaker. Remember, fluency is built step by step, habit by habit.

Next up, we'll dive into the *Feedback* section of the MKPF framework. Practice sets the stage, but feedback is what sharpens your skills even further. It's time to see how real-time corrections and insights can fuel your growth. So, get ready to embrace the feedback process and take your speaking to the next level. The journey continues!

> *Don't just learn language—live it.*

Feedback

Welcome to the fourth and final pillar of the Confluent Speaker Framework (MKPF)—**Feedback**. You've worked on your mindset, built your knowledge, and practiced consistently. But without feedback, you'll be like a ship sailing with no clear destination—lost and without direction.

Feedback is like your exam results. It shows you where you stand, highlights the areas you're excelling in, and points out the blind spots that you can't see but others can. It brings you clarity, showing you what's working and what needs improvement.

In the following chapters, we'll dive deeper into why feedback is crucial to your speaking journey and how to get it from a variety of sources—whether it's from your peers, mentors, or even from yourself.

I want to start by sharing a personal story about feedback. I, too, am always looking for feedback on my own communication skills. One day, one of my learners told me, "Sir, you speak too fast." At first, I was taken aback. But then I did what I encourage all my learners to do—*I asked for more feedback*. I went to other batches and asked them if they felt the same way. It turned out, they did.

So, I took that feedback seriously. I slowed down my pace during sessions, consciously working to make sure my learners could follow me better. After a month, I asked them again how my pace was, and this time, they said it was much better and easier to understand. This marked a successful application of feedback and a change I made because I accepted and applied what I had been told.

The power of feedback is that it provides insights we can't always see ourselves. As humans, we can be emotionally attached to our own ideas, to our speaking style, to our "perfect" language. It's hard to separate ourselves from our work and look at it with clear eyes. But the beauty of feedback is that it's objective. People around us—whether it's our learners, mentors, or colleagues—can give us an honest, unemotional perspective on our progress.

In my sessions, I regularly point out mistakes in grammar, pronunciation, and filler words. Many times, learners are quick to deny these errors, saying, "No, I didn't say that!" But instead of arguing, I wait for the moment when they repeat that mistake, and I highlight it in real-time. This is when the learner realizes that, even though they were making the mistake, they didn't notice it themselves.

When we speak, we're often too focused on structure, grammar, pronunciation, and our reputation to notice the small errors—like fillers, or subtle mispronunciations. That's where regular feedback helps. It acts as a mirror, reflecting back to you what you can't see.

Once you start incorporating regular feedback into your routine, you'll notice its profound impact on your growth. Feedback is a tool for improvement that you can't ignore. In fact, you should strive to make seeking feedback a lifelong habit. Whether it's from mentors, colleagues, or even friends, everyone needs someone who can give them genuine, honest feedback to help them grow.

Feedback will not only refine your speaking skills but also open doors for you to become the confident and fluent speaker you're aiming to be.

In the upcoming chapters, we'll explore **why feedback is so important** and **how to get it from various sources**—so you can continue improving, learning, and moving forward on your journey to fluency. Stay tuned.

CHAPTER 30

Why a Guru?

One day, I asked my best friend, "What's the most important life lesson you've learned?" His reply has stuck with me ever since. He said, "Har Arjun ko apni zindagi mein ek Krishna dhundhna chahiye." (Every Arjuna should find their Krishna in life.)

This hit me hard. It made me realize how important it is to have the right mentor—someone who accelerates your growth. But when I say "guru," I don't necessarily mean a language teacher. A guru can be anyone you trust—someone who's ahead of you in the area you want to improve in, someone who can point out mistakes you can't see, someone who understands your struggles, your aspirations, and your dreams.

I've had many gurus in my own life. My first guru was my father. He shaped me into who I am today, and words cannot express how much his support and guidance have meant to me. My second guru was a lady who gave me the opportunity to step into the world of language teaching by offering me a job as her assistant. With her guidance and feedback, I climbed the ladder of success. And even now, my wife corrects my pronunciation and helps me refine my language skills.

But my learning hasn't stopped there. I have had the privilege of learning from many of my students as well. I've been fortunate to work with individuals from diverse fields—fashion designers, IT professionals, lawyers, engineers, and even politicians. Each one of them, in their own way, has been a guru to me. They share their world knowledge, their experiences, and their perspectives, which enrich my understanding and broaden my own outlook. These gurus, with their unique expertise, have helped me see the world in ways I never could have imagined. Whether it's understanding the creative world of fashion or navigating the technicalities of law and IT, they've shown me how vast and varied life truly is.

We all need a guru—a guide. And no, I'm not saying I am the only guru out there. You should seek guidance from different people around you—your cousins, your friends, your colleagues—people who care about you, understand your goals, and are better at certain things than you are. Get feedback from those who can see what you cannot. They will help you grow faster than you ever imagined.

The point is, feedback from a trusted guru can unlock your potential and help you refine your skills in ways you can't do alone. So, don't hesitate—seek out people who will push you to be your best, who understand where you're coming from, and who will give you honest, constructive feedback.

> *Your fluency is already in you—just let it speak!*

CHAPTER 31

The Power of Constructive Feedback

Let's talk about constructive feedback. It's like having a mirror that doesn't just reflect your flaws but also shows you how to fix them. This kind of feedback is the secret weapon in your journey toward becoming a confident and fluent speaker.

Now, here's the thing—feedback isn't always easy to take. Sometimes it stings, doesn't it? But here's what I've learned: feedback is never your enemy. If it's constructive, it's your greatest ally.

Why Constructive Feedback Works

There's a difference between someone telling you, "That was wrong," and someone saying, "Here's what you can do to make it better." One leaves you frustrated, while the other makes you feel like there's hope.

For example, let's say you're working on your pronunciation. If someone tells you, "Your pronunciation isn't good," that's not helpful—it's just negative feedback. But if they say, "You're pronouncing 'comfortable' wrong; it's pronounced as 'kumf-tur-bul.' Let's try it together," now that's constructive. It's clear, actionable, and designed to help you improve.

My Journey with Feedback

I've received my fair share of feedback over the years. Some of it was tough to hear, but it changed my life. In fact, I wouldn't be where I am today without it.

When I first started teaching, I had no idea what I was doing. My first mentor gave me honest feedback about my lessons. "You're too fast, Zia," she'd say. "You need to slow down and give people time to absorb what you're saying." At first, it felt like she was pointing out my flaws. But with time, I realized she was giving me the tools to become better.

Even now, I rely on feedback. Some of the most valuable feedback comes from unexpected sources— like my participants. You all come from such diverse fields—fashion, IT, law, engineering, politics—and every session teaches me something new about the world. Your insights, questions, and even challenges have shaped me as a coach.

How to Embrace Feedback

Here's the golden rule: Don't fear feedback. It's not here to embarrass you; it's here to help you grow. I know it can feel personal sometimes, especially if it's pointing out something you've struggled with for a while. But instead of letting it pull you down, let it push you forward.

When someone gives you constructive feedback:

1. **Listen fully**: Don't interrupt or start defending yourself. Just take it in.

2. **Ask questions**: If you don't understand the feedback, ask for clarification.

3. **Apply it**: The feedback won't help if you don't act on it. Put it into practice right away.

And most importantly, don't let your ego get in the way. If someone cares enough to give you constructive feedback, they're invested in your growth.

> *Your voice is not waiting for grammar—it's waiting for courage.*

CHAPTER 32

Growth, Not Perfection

You've probably heard me say this before, but fluency is a journey, not a destination. It's not about being perfect; it's about improving step by step. Constructive feedback helps you identify those steps. It's like a map for your progress.

Think of it this way: When you go to the gym, the trainer doesn't just say, "You're weak." They say, "Here's how you can strengthen your muscles. Start with lighter weights, then gradually increase." The same goes for language. Feedback helps you build those mental and verbal muscles.

How to Find Constructive Feedback

Feedback can come from anywhere. It doesn't have to be from a teacher. Your friends, colleagues, or even family members can be great sources. Find people who care about your progress and have the knowledge to guide you.

And hey, don't forget technology! AI tools like chatbots and language apps can give you feedback on pronunciation, grammar, and more. (We'll dive deeper into this in a later chapter.)

Final Thoughts

Constructive feedback isn't criticism—it's a gift. It's someone saying, "I see your potential, and I want to help you reach it." When you shift your mindset to see feedback as an opportunity instead of a judgment, you unlock a new level of growth.

Remember, every piece of feedback—whether it's from me, your peers, or even a random comment from a friend—has the power to make you better. But only if you embrace it.

So, next time someone offers you feedback, don't shy away. Lean in, listen, and let it shape you into the **Confluent Speaker** you're meant to be. Keep learning, keep growing, and keep speaking with confidence. The journey continues!

> *You don't become fluent by knowing English; you become fluent by using it.*

CHAPTER 33

How to Accept Feedback Without Ego

Let's be real—accepting feedback isn't always easy. Sometimes it feels like someone is pointing a spotlight at your flaws, and your first instinct might be to defend yourself or ignore what they're saying. But here's the truth: feedback is never about tearing you down; it's about building you up. And to grow, you need to leave your ego at the door.

Why Feedback Feels Personal

When someone gives us feedback, it's natural to feel defensive. You might think, *Are they questioning my abilities? Don't they see how much effort I've put in?* But this is where the challenge lies—learning to separate your work or performance from your identity.

Feedback isn't about who you are; it's about where you can go. It's not a judgment of your worth but an opportunity to unlock your potential.

Why Accepting Feedback Matters

Here's the thing: if you can't take feedback, you can't grow. It's as simple as that. The best athletes, performers, and speakers didn't become great because they were perfect from the start. They became great because they had people pointing out what wasn't working—and they listened.

Imagine this: You're speaking in English, and someone points out a common mistake you make with verb tenses. Yes, it might feel a bit awkward at the moment, but that one piece of feedback could stop you from making the same mistake in every conversation.

How to Accept Feedback Gracefully

Let me share some tips that have worked for me:

1. **Pause Before Reacting:** When someone gives you feedback, resist the urge to respond immediately. Take a deep breath, listen carefully, and let their words sink in. It's easy to react defensively, but a moment of pause can help you respond with maturity.

2. **Shift Your Perspective:** Instead of thinking, *Why are they criticizing me?* ask yourself, *What can I learn from this?* Feedback isn't about tearing you down; it's about lifting you up.

3. **Say Thank You:** This one is tough but powerful. When someone takes the time to give you feedback, thank them—even if it's hard to hear. They're investing in your growth.

4. **Ask Questions:** If you don't fully understand the feedback, ask for clarification. For example, if someone says, "You need to work on your

pronunciation," ask, "Could you give me an example of what I'm mispronouncing?" The more specific the feedback, the more actionable it becomes.

5. **Apply What You Learn:** Feedback means nothing if you don't act on it. Take notes, practice, and show that you're serious about improving.

The Role of Emotional Maturity

Accepting feedback without ego is a sign of emotional maturity. It shows that you're more focused on growth than on defending your current self. It's about recognizing that you're a work in progress—and that's a good thing.

Think about it: the people giving you feedback (whether it's me, your colleagues, or even technology) don't want you to fail. They want to see you succeed. They see your potential, and their feedback is a way of helping you reach it.

A Personal Reflection

I'll admit, I've struggled with feedback in the past too. Early in my career, when someone pointed out flaws in my teaching style, I'd take it personally. I'd think, *They don't understand how hard I'm trying.* But over time, I realized something important: their feedback wasn't a criticism of my effort; it was a roadmap for improvement.

Some of the best lessons I've learned came from feedback I didn't want to hear. My pronunciation errors, my pacing, even the way I structured my sessions—these were all areas I improved because someone cared enough to point them out.

Final Thoughts

Feedback isn't your enemy—your ego is. When you let go of the need to be perfect and embrace the fact that you're a learner, feedback becomes a gift, not a threat.

So, the next time someone offers you feedback, remind yourself: it's not personal, it's progress. Thank them, reflect on their words, and put their advice into action. That's how you grow—not just as a speaker, but as a person.

And remember, every time you accept feedback with grace, you're one step closer to becoming the confident, fluent communicator you're meant to be. Keep going—you've got this!

> *Every sentence spoken is a step toward your future self.*

CHAPTER 34

Not All Feedback is Useful

The best and worst part about feedback is that feedback is everywhere. Friends, family, colleagues, even strangers will have opinions about what you're doing and how you're doing it. While some of it can be golden, not all feedback is worth taking to heart. In fact, trying to apply every piece of advice can leave you confused and overwhelmed.

Here's the truth: not all feedback aligns with your goals or serves your growth. Some feedback comes from people who genuinely want to help, while other feedback might come from those who don't fully understand your journey. And that's okay. Your job is to filter what's useful and let the rest go.

When you're deciding whether to act on feedback, ask yourself: *Does this align with my vision? Is it coming from someone who understands my goals?* If the answer is yes, take it seriously and work on it. But if the feedback feels random or off-track, don't let it distract you. Respect the intention behind it, but stay focused on your path.

Remember, the most valuable feedback will help you improve without pulling you away from what matters most to you. Trust yourself to know the difference. After all, you're the one steering this ship, and not every wave is worth chasing. Stay true to your journey.

> *Don't chase perfect English—chase real expression.*

CHAPTER 35

Seeking Feedback in Real Time

The best time to get feedback? Right when the moment is fresh. Think about it—feedback hits differently when it's tied directly to what just happened. If you wait too long, the details blur, and the impact of the feedback gets diluted.

Whether it's after a presentation, a conversation, or even a practice session, make it a habit to ask for feedback immediately. For example, if you're practicing your speaking skills, ask, "Did I come across clearly?" or "Was my pronunciation okay?" right after you finish. People are more likely to remember specifics and offer insights that are relevant and actionable.

Real-time feedback is powerful because it allows you to make instant adjustments. You'll start noticing small shifts—correcting fillers, improving clarity, or tweaking your tone—all in the moment. It's like refining your skills on the go, making you sharper with each step.

Don't be afraid to ask questions like, "What could I improve?" or "Was there anything unclear?" These open the door to honest and constructive input. And when you apply that feedback right away, you'll not only grow faster but also build trust with those giving you feedback—they'll see you value their insights.

Remember, feedback in real time is like a live compass—it keeps you on track and guides you to improvement without delay. Don't wait. Seek it, use it, and grow from it while the moment is still alive.

> *Clarity is more powerful than complexity.*

CHAPTER 36

The Feedback Loop: Apply, Test, Improve

Feedback isn't something you check off a to-do list. It's a process—a loop that keeps going as long as you're open to learning. You get feedback, apply it, test your improvement, and then seek feedback again. That's how real growth happens.

Think about it: You receive a suggestion, like improving your pronunciation or reducing fillers. You start applying it during your conversations. But here's the key—you don't stop there. You test it. You pay attention to how people respond. You ask, "Did this feel clearer? Am I making progress?" Their input becomes the next step in your loop.

This cycle ensures that you're not just hearing feedback but truly using it to evolve. It's about refining, experimenting, and constantly leveling up. Over time, you'll notice not only improvement but also confidence in areas where you once struggled.

Remember, feedback isn't a one-and-done deal. It's a continuous process, like sharpening a blade—you work on it bit by bit until it's razor-sharp. Embrace the loop, and let it guide you toward your best self, one improvement at a time.

> *Speak as if the world needs your story—because it does.*

CHAPTER 37

Feedback from Different Sources

Imagine seeing yourself through multiple mirrors, each reflecting a different angle of who you are. That's what feedback from different sources does—it gives you a 360-degree view of your strengths and areas for improvement.

Your mentor might focus on your overall growth. Your peers might notice habits or patterns you don't see in yourself. Colleagues could give insights on how you communicate in a professional setting. Even family can provide feedback—they know you deeply and can point out things others might miss.

The beauty of gathering feedback from diverse sources is that it fills in the blind spots. It helps you understand how you're perceived in different contexts and what you can work on to become more effective and impactful.

But here's the thing: not all feedback will align or make sense immediately. That's okay. Take what resonates, analyze recurring themes, and let them guide your improvement.

When you create this web of feedback, you build a fuller picture of your abilities and growth areas. It's not about pleasing everyone; it's about evolving with clarity and purpose. Let the voices of those who care about your success guide you toward becoming the best version of yourself.

> *Confidence isn't loud—it's consistent.*

CHAPTER 38

Using Ai for Real-Time Language Feedback

In today's world, technology can be a game-changer when it comes to improving your language skills. AI-driven tools, such as speech recognition and grammar checkers, provide you with instant feedback on your pronunciation, grammar, and sentence structure—right in the moment. This means you can make quick adjustments as you speak or write, without waiting for someone else to tell you what needs improvement.

Using AI tools can be like having a language coach in your pocket. There are many apps and software out there designed to help you assess your language skills in real time. They'll point out errors you might miss and offer suggestions on how to improve. The best part? You get the opportunity to fix those mistakes immediately, so you're continuously refining your language abilities.

Make AI a regular part of your practice. Let it support you in your journey to become a confident and fluent speaker, helping you develop quicker and smarter. Technology, when used right, can be a powerful tool to speed up your learning and give you the instant feedback you need to progress.

> *Fluency blooms in conversations, not in classrooms.*

CHAPTER 39

Voice Analysis Tools: Ai for Pronunciation Feedback

AI-powered voice analysis tools are taking language learning to the next level by helping you fine-tune your pronunciation. These tools go beyond the basics and can pick up on even the smallest nuances in how you speak—nuances that might be overlooked by a human listener. From evaluating the rhythm of your speech to checking your stress patterns and intonation, these tools offer detailed feedback that helps you refine every aspect of your pronunciation.

Voice analysis tools provide a unique opportunity to identify specific pronunciation errors you may not even realize you're making. They don't just tell you you're wrong; they explain exactly what needs to be adjusted. This means you can work on the finer details of your pronunciation and make corrections quickly, leading to much more accurate and confident speech.

Using these AI tools regularly can accelerate your improvement, especially if you're focused on getting those tricky sounds or accents just right. Let these tools guide you through the process of refining your voice—one feedback session at a time.

> *The faster you forgive your mistakes, the faster you grow.*

CHAPTER 40

Turning Negative Feedback Into Actionable Steps

Negative feedback stings, doesn't it? No one likes to hear what they're doing wrong, but here's the truth: some of the most valuable lessons hide in that discomfort. Negative feedback isn't an attack—it's an invitation to grow.

The key is to separate emotions from the message. Instead of focusing on how the feedback made you feel, focus on what you can learn from it. If someone points out that your presentations lack clarity, don't take it as a judgment on your intelligence. Instead, ask yourself, *What can I do to make my ideas clearer?*

Turn that vague critique into specific actions. Maybe you need to work on structuring your ideas better or practicing your delivery. Break the feedback down into steps you can actually implement. Then, commit to improving one piece at a time.

Here's the magic of this approach: when you act on negative feedback, you're proving to yourself that you can handle challenges and rise above them. Over time, what once felt like criticism starts to feel like a roadmap to becoming better. And that's a powerful shift.

So, the next time someone points out a flaw, don't let it discourage you. Let it guide you. Take that feedback, turn it into a plan, and let it fuel your growth.

> *Progress sounds messy—that's how you know it's real.*

Creating a Feedback-Friendly Environment

If you want honest, constructive feedback, the first step is to make sure people feel safe enough to give it. Feedback thrives in an environment of trust and openness. When others know they won't be judged or criticized for their opinions, they're more likely to share their thoughts with you—and you're more likely to hear the truth that will help you grow.

Start by encouraging open communication. Let people know you value their input and are genuinely seeking ways to improve. Avoid reacting defensively when you receive feedback, even if it's tough to hear. Instead, listen intently and express gratitude for their honesty.

A safe space isn't just about making others feel comfortable; it's about building trust and showing that you're open to learning. When feedback feels like a two-way street, where everyone is respected and valued, it becomes a powerful tool for growth. So, create an atmosphere where feedback is welcomed, not feared. That's when real growth happens.

Grammar doesn't drive fluency—bravery does.

CHAPTER 42

Self-Feedback: The Art of Self-Reflection

Self-feedback is one of the most powerful tools for growth because it gives you the ability to assess your own performance and make improvements without always relying on others. Being able to step back and reflect on your actions, your speech, and your progress is essential for becoming a truly independent learner.

Start by being brutally honest with yourself. After a presentation, a conversation, or any task, take a moment to think about what went well and what didn't. Ask yourself, "What can I improve? What should I keep doing?" Don't shy away from areas where you feel less confident. These are the places where your growth lies.

Developing the habit of self-reflection will not only help you act on the feedback you receive from others but will also empower you to take charge of your learning. Combine your self-feedback with the constructive input from others, and you'll see a dramatic difference in how quickly you can grow. Self-feedback is your internal guide that keeps you aligned with your goals.

(See appendix for a list of self-feedback questions)

> *Even one word spoken with courage is more powerful than a hundred left unspoken.*

The Road Ahead for You as a Confluent Speaker

As we come to the close of this book, it's important to take a step back and look at the bigger picture. Becoming a Confluent Speaker isn't a quick fix, nor is it about reaching a final destination. It's about starting a journey, one that will take you through moments of growth, challenges, and breakthroughs. In this section, we'll talk about the prize—what it really means to speak with confidence and fluency. We'll explore how you can keep the fire alive and stay motivated through the highs and lows, and most importantly, how to live as a Confluent Speaker. Fluency, after all, is a lifestyle, not just a goal. So, let's dive into these next chapters and continue building the mindset and habits that will sustain your progress and success, one conversation at a time.

CHAPTER 43

The Prize

The Moment When Your Speaking Becomes Natural and Fluent

This is what you get when you follow the Confluent Speaker Framework (MKPF)—the moment when speaking English feels like second nature. Imagine speaking without having to pause or search for words, where your thoughts flow effortlessly into speech, and you feel completely confident in any conversation, big or small. That's the prize.

What's special about this system is that it's not just about learning grammar or memorizing vocabulary. It's about giving you a clear structure—a system you can always rely on. The four key areas—**Mindset, Knowledge, Practice, and Feedback**—are what you'll focus on. These four pillars will guide you, and the beauty of it is that you can always assess yourself in these areas. You'll know where you're strong and where you need to keep improving, and you'll never be lost about what to do next.

Once you have this framework, you'll have a systematic approach to work on your speaking every day. No more random, unfocused learning. You'll always know what areas to work on, and how to improve. Plus, I'll share with you "scene-shifting" questions that will change how you think about language and communication. These will help you see your progress, and push you to the next level, time and again.

And the best part? You'll have the right mindset. You'll understand that fluency isn't something you achieve once and for all. It's a journey, a continuous path of growth. By following this approach, you'll change your perception of how you speak, how you learn, and how you approach any conversation. You'll become someone who speaks with confidence, and who has the tools to keep improving.

This framework doesn't just make you fluent—it makes you a Confluent Speaker, someone who knows how to communicate with ease, clarity, and power, in any situation, for the rest of your life.

> *To speak well, speak often—even if it's awkward.*

CHAPTER 44

Sustaining Motivation: Keep the Fire Alive

Staying motivated on this journey isn't always easy. But remember, you're not alone, and I've got your back. To keep you on track, I've shared a list of Confluent Commandments at the end of this book. These commandments are your guiding principles—reminders that will help you stay motivated, keep moving forward, and stay focused on what truly matters.

Each commandment has been crafted to help you build a mindset that thrives on growth, not perfection. When you're feeling stuck or uncertain, just turn to them, and they'll help reignite that fire and keep you going. Trust me, if you follow these commandments, you'll always have the motivation to keep improving and speaking your way to fluency.

> *Your accent is your identity, not your inadequacy.*

CHAPTER 45

Living as a Confluent Speaker: confidence is a Way of Life—Not a Goal

Being a Confluent Speaker isn't about reaching a certain destination; it's about living the journey every single day. Confidence isn't a one-time achievement that you check off and move on from. It's a mindset that you build and carry with you, constantly evolving as you grow.

When you begin to see confidence as a lifestyle, you start to show up differently in conversations. You stop waiting for the "perfect moment" or the "right circumstances." Instead, you start speaking with intention, embracing the uncertainty, and focusing on connecting rather than perfecting.

Fluency and confidence go hand in hand. As you speak more, you'll find that your confidence grows naturally, not just in English but in your ability to express yourself in any situation. So, living as a Confluent Speaker means living with the understanding that confidence comes from taking action, from showing up, and from embracing the process, not from waiting for the perfect set of circumstances.

This is where the real transformation happens. Confidence becomes part of who you are, not something you have to work towards. When you live as a Confluent Speaker, you aren't just fluent—you're fearless. You speak because you believe in your message, and that belief shines through in every word you say.

> *Fluency is not about being ready—it's about being willing.*

CHAPTER 46

Fluency is a Lifelong Journey

Fluency is not something you "arrive" at and then stop. It's not a place where you can sit back and relax, thinking, "I've made it." It's a habit—an ongoing journey that evolves with every conversation, every new experience, and every challenge you take on.

Just like fitness, fluency requires consistent practice. The more you speak, the more natural it becomes, and the better you get at navigating conversations with ease. But here's the secret: fluency isn't about perfection. It's about progress. It's about showing up every day, speaking, making mistakes, learning, and growing.

If you want to sustain your fluency, you need to keep it alive. Don't think of fluency as a goal that ends once you speak "perfectly." Think of it as a living, breathing habit that you continue to nurture. As you keep practicing, you'll find yourself becoming a more confident and resourceful speaker—because fluency, like any other skill, is a result of continuous effort and learning.

So, remember: fluency isn't a fixed point you reach, it's a continuous journey. And as long as you keep going, you'll keep getting better, growing, and connecting. The beauty of fluency is that it never stops—it becomes a part of you, something you carry throughout your life.

> *The fluency you seek is hidden inside the words you're afraid to say.*

CHAPTER 47

Come to It When It Comes to You

Once you read this book, you'll start to notice something powerful — certain chapters, ideas, or even sentences will come back to you at different stages of your life. This isn't a coincidence. It's a sign that your subconscious is working in the background, analyzing, processing, and evaluating the insights you've absorbed.

If you're aware enough, you'll catch yourself being reminded of specific parts of this book, maybe even at unexpected moments. When this happens, **go back** to that chapter. **Revisit** it. This isn't just about reading; it's about deepening your understanding. The first time you read it, it was information. But now, with experience and reflection, that same information will hold a deeper meaning. You'll discover new layers of insight.

This is how learning works. Think about how you learned to ride a bike or drive a car. The first time, it was awkward, clumsy. But as you gained experience, things became easier, more automatic. Every time you did it, even just a little bit, it became smoother. And over time, it got better and better.

I've noticed this with the old cab drivers in Mumbai. You've probably seen them — the "uncles" driving the taxis. They may not seem particularly active, but their driving is so smooth, you could be in an old Omni and still feel like you're in a Rolls Royce. That's the beauty of experience. It's not always about speed, but about effortless mastery — the ability to handle something with grace and ease because you've been through it, over and over.

So, when a chapter from this book comes back to you — whether days, weeks, or months from now — it's not just a coincidence. It's a sign that your learning is deepening, and you're moving toward mastery. **When it comes to you, come to it.**

> *Don't pause for permission—speak your truth into the world.*

Moving Beyond the Book

This book is only the beginning. Now that you've uncovered the framework and gained insights into becoming a Confluent Speaker, the real work begins. It's time to take action, build momentum, and carve your own path. Fluency is not something that's handed to you—it's something you create, step by step, conversation by conversation.

In this next section, we'll dive deeper into how you can sustain your progress, design your own personalized learning journey, and take the valuable lessons you've learned to inspire and help others. You'll learn how to continue building on your confidence and fluency long after you've finished reading. It's time to stop reading and start speaking.

Through these chapters, I'll share practical advice on keeping your growth alive, designing a learning path that works for you, and even using your own journey to help others. Your fluency is just the beginning of something much bigger—a lifelong habit that continues to evolve and grow. Let's get started on making this journey your own.

CHAPTER 48

Sustaining Your Progress Beyond This Book

You've come a long way, but the journey doesn't stop here. The key to keeping your progress alive is consistency. You've gained the foundation, now it's time to build your own unique path forward. The momentum you've gained through the Confluent Speaker Framework can be sustained with a few simple yet powerful strategies.

Start by creating a habit of speaking. It doesn't matter if it's a formal conversation, a casual chat, or speaking out loud to yourself. Speak whenever you get the chance. Keep your focus on the four pillars—Mindset, Knowledge, Practice, and Feedback—because they'll continue to guide you as you move forward.

If you fall off track, that's okay. Don't beat yourself up. Just pick yourself up, reflect on your progress, and keep going. You'll have days where it feels like you're not improving, but those days are just part of the process. The important thing is to stay engaged, to keep challenging yourself, and to keep learning.

Look at language as a living thing that's growing with you. Don't wait for the perfect moment to speak, because that moment doesn't exist. Speak as much as you can, embrace mistakes, and be kind to yourself through the process.

As you continue, remember: this isn't about reaching a destination; it's about maintaining the momentum and continuing to evolve.

> *Real fluency begins when you stop apologizing for your voice.*

CHAPTER 49

Creating Your Own Learning Path

You are the architect of your language journey. The beauty of learning a new language—especially the Confluent way—is that it's completely in your hands. No one knows you better than yourself, so take charge of your progress and design a path that works for you.

Start by reflecting on what excites you the most. Is it real conversations? Reading books? Watching movies? Choose methods that you enjoy and integrate them into your daily routine. Make language learning something you *want* to do, not something you *have* to do. When learning becomes fun, you'll naturally stay motivated.

Now, break down your journey into smaller, achievable steps. Set your own milestones, but remember, they don't have to be huge leaps. Small wins every day build up over time. It's not about perfection—it's about making steady progress.

Also, keep revisiting the four pillars: Mindset, Knowledge, Practice, and Feedback. You'll need to adjust these pillars as you evolve. For example, as you grow in confidence, your mindset may shift, and you might focus more on mastering specific vocabulary or accent. Use the framework as a guide, but let it evolve with you.

You're not bound by a rigid syllabus or a fixed timeline. In fact, learning doesn't have to be linear. Some days you'll focus more on speaking, other days on listening, and that's perfectly fine. The goal is to keep moving forward, continuously finding ways to challenge yourself.

Create your path with flexibility, excitement, and passion. You are the learner, the teacher, and the guide on this journey. Enjoy the ride, and remember—you control the pace, the direction, and the way you learn.

> *The only way out of fear is through it—word by word.*

CHAPTER 50

Stop Reading, Start Speaking

Enough reading. Enough planning. Now it's time to *speak*. This book is just the start. The real work begins when you start using what you've learned. Fluency doesn't come from consuming information—it comes from taking action.

Every moment you hesitate, you delay your growth. Speak now, even if it's messy. Speak without overthinking. The more you speak, the more fluent you become. The road to confidence is paved with conversations, not pages.

Put down the book, step into the real world, and make your voice heard. Don't wait for the "perfect moment." It's now. Start speaking, and everything else will follow.

> *You don't need more vocabulary—you need more courage to use what you have.*

CHAPTER 51

Paying It Forward—Helping Others Become Confluent

This journey doesn't end with you. Once you've broken through your own barriers, found your confidence, and become a fluent speaker, it's time to do what others did for you. It's time to pay it forward.

I'm someone who started with a Hindi medium background. I wasn't born speaking English fluently. But people helped me. They believed in me. They pushed me. And today, I'm here helping you break through those same barriers.

You know what? It's your turn now. Once you've reached a place of fluency, help someone else get there. Push your brother, sister, even your mom, dad, colleagues, and friends. Tell them to grow. Tell them to take those efforts. Be the guiding light that someone was for you. Show them that if you can do it, so can they. The moment you start guiding someone, you'll realize how much more you've grown.

It's not just about speaking well—it's about passing on that belief, that mindset, and that action to others. Be the person who pulls someone up when they're struggling, just like someone did for you.

Trust me, the feeling you get from helping others grow is unmatched. And together, we'll create a community of fluent, confident speakers who inspire each other every step of the way.

> *Every 'wrong' sentence is a right step forward.*

Appendix

Scene-Shifting Questions

In this section, we dive into what I call **Scene-Shifting Questions**. These are questions that act like a spotlight, illuminating new perspectives and challenging the way you think about your speaking journey. Just like in a movie, where the scene changes and a fresh outlook opens up, these questions will help you shift from one way of thinking to another, allowing you to break free from limiting beliefs and step into a new mindset.

Scene-Shifting Questions are designed to shift your mindset, encourage growth, and provoke clarity. By answering them regularly, you can begin to see your English learning journey from a different angle—one where your challenges become your strengths, your fears transform into opportunities, and your journey becomes more about progress than perfection.

These questions may feel counterintuitive at first, but that's exactly why they're so powerful. They lead you to breakthrough moments where you start to understand that *you already have what it takes*. Embrace them, ask them to yourself often, and watch how your perspective changes, bringing you closer to becoming a truly confident, independent speaker.

Here's how they work:

1. **They shift your perspective.** Many learners see fluency as a distant mountain to climb. These questions help you realize you're already on the mountain—you've just been looking at the wrong peak.

2. **They reframe challenges as opportunities.** Fear, mistakes, and uncertainty are not signs of failure. They're evidence that you're growing and evolving.

3. **They help you own your strengths.** Too often, we downplay what we're already good at. These questions push you to recognize and build on your unique abilities.

4. **They provoke action.** When your mindset shifts, your actions naturally follow. You'll stop hesitating and start experimenting, speaking, and learning with confidence.

Think of these as **coaching in your pocket.** Ask yourself these questions regularly—especially when you feel stuck or unsure. Write down your answers. Reflect on them. And most importantly, allow them to do what they're meant to: **make you think differently.**

This is not just about improving your English. It's about reshaping how you see yourself as a speaker, a communicator, and even as a person. The goal? To help you step into your most confident, fluent self—not someday, but starting today.

Now, take a deep breath, turn the page, and get ready to meet the questions that could change everything.

The scene-shifting questions

1. Challenging Self-Perception

> ➤ What if you're already more fluent than you believe? How would that change your approach to speaking?

> ➤ If you were to consider your speaking challenges as strengths, what would those strengths be?

2. Reframing Emotions

> ➤ How might feeling anxious about speaking indicate that you care deeply about your communication?

> ➤ What if making mistakes was the key to becoming a more confident speaker rather than a setback?

3. Visualizing Alternative Identities

> ➤ If you viewed yourself as a natural communicator rather than a learner, what new habits would you adopt?

> ➤ Imagine a world where fluency isn't the goal—what would you focus on instead when speaking English?

4. Disrupting Limitations

- ➢ How could viewing yourself as a beginner actually empower you to take more risks in speaking?

- ➢ What if your biggest fear about speaking was actually a sign that you're on the brink of a breakthrough?

5. Exploring Personal Strengths

- ➢ If you had to teach someone else how to communicate confidently, what would you advise them, even if you don't follow that advice yourself?

- ➢ How might your perceived weaknesses actually provide unique perspectives or insights in conversation?

6. Setting Intentions for Uncertainty

- ➢ What if embracing uncertainty in speaking led to greater opportunities than striving for perfection?

- ➢ How could accepting that you might never feel fully "fluent" free you to communicate more openly and authentically?

7. Contradicting Common Beliefs

- ➢ What if speaking in English is less about language skills and more about connecting with others? How would that shift your priorities?

- ➢ If you believed that fluency is irrelevant to making an impact, how would you change your speaking style?

8. Reimagining Growth

- ➢ How might thinking of your speaking journey as a never-ending adventure change the way you engage in conversations?

- ➢ What if your current level of English is the perfect starting point for inspiring others? How does that change your role in conversations?

> *Perfection is silent. Progress speaks.*

Self Feedback Questions

Self-Feedback Questions: A Guide for Reflection and Growth

These questions are designed to help you reflect on your speaking and communication skills after a conversation or speaking activity. Use them as a tool to guide your learning and help you identify areas for improvement. The more specific and honest you are, the more effective your self-reflection will be.

Before the Conversation/Activity

1. What are my goals for this conversation? What do I want to accomplish?

2. How prepared am I for this conversation (vocabulary, topic knowledge, etc.)?

3. Am I confident and calm? What mindset am I bringing into this interaction?

During the Conversation/Activity

4. Was I able to express my thoughts clearly? What words or phrases felt difficult to say?

5. How well did I listen and understand what the other person said?

6. Did I stay focused and stay on topic, or did I get distracted?

7. Was my body language open and confident? Did I make eye contact?

8. Did I notice any nervous habits, like speaking too fast, stuttering, or using fillers?

After the Conversation/Activity

9. What went well during the conversation? What am I proud of?

10. What areas felt challenging or uncomfortable? Why?

11. Did I manage to convey my message effectively, or was there a breakdown in communication?

12. What new vocabulary or phrases did I learn and use?

13. Was I able to handle mistakes and recover smoothly?

14. Did I feel confident overall, or did I let my nerves take over?

15. How did the other person respond to me? Did they seem engaged or confused?

Looking Forward

16. What can I improve next time? (Focus on one area for growth)

17. How can I better prepare for similar conversations in the future?

18. What feedback from others (if any) should I incorporate into my practice?

19. How can I make my communication clearer, more concise, or more engaging?

20. What progress have I made from previous conversations?

Bonus Questions for Deeper Reflection

21. How did I handle moments of uncertainty or self-doubt during the conversation?

22. How can I use feedback (from others or self-reflection) to adjust my approach next time?

23. What have I learned about my speaking habits that I can work on?

24. What is one thing I can do today to practice and improve before my next speaking opportunity?

How to Use These Questions

Take some time after each conversation or speaking activity to answer a few or all of these questions. You can write your answers in a journal, on your phone, or in a digital note. Doing this regularly will help you notice patterns in your speaking habits and pinpoint areas that need work. Use these insights to create an actionable plan for improvement in your next speaking practice session.

How Often to Use It: Use this self-reflection tool after every significant speaking opportunity, whether it's a practice session, a meeting, or a casual conversation. Regular reflection will help you stay on track with your goals and accelerate your progress.

By making self-reflection a habit, you'll be able to keep growing and improving every time you speak.

> *You're not learning English; you're learning to express yourself.*

7 Signs of a Confluent Speaker

Are you a confident speaker?

Every time you speak, you have the opportunity to inspire, connect, and make an impact. But what truly defines a confident speaker? It's not just about fluency or perfect grammar; it's about embodying certain qualities that resonate with authenticity and confidence. Let's explore the essential traits that make you a confident speaker:

1. **Authenticity**: When you speak from the heart, staying true to who you are, you connect on a deeper level with others. Your authentic voice holds the power to create real, lasting impact.

2. **Confidence**: A confident speaker isn't afraid to share their unique perspective. Confidence shines when you embrace who you are and speak up, regardless of any doubts.

3. **Growth Mindset**: Challenges? You don't see them as roadblocks; you see them as opportunities. You are always seeking ways to improve, evolve, and grow, which makes you a dynamic speaker.

4. **Effective Communication**: The ability to clearly and engagingly express your ideas is what sets you

apart. Fluency isn't the measure—it's how well you can connect your thoughts to others.

5. **Emotional Intelligence**: A confident speaker knows how to read the room and adapt their message to resonate emotionally with their audience. It's about more than just words—it's about feeling.

6. **Resilience**: You keep going. No matter how many setbacks or mistakes you face, you rise, speak up, and continue sharing your voice.

7. **Passion**: When you speak about what lights you up, you inspire others. Passion is contagious. When you speak with enthusiasm, you motivate and empower those around you.

Remember, being a confident speaker isn't about perfection; it's about connection. If you see any of these traits in yourself, know that you are already on your way to becoming a confident speaker. Celebrate your journey, embrace your voice, and continue growing. The world is waiting to hear what you have to say!

You're not just speaking; you're changing the conversation. Keep going.

> *Speak not to impress, but to connect.*

The Confluent Score: Your Personal Fluency Game

How It Works

1. Self-Assessment

For each of the 6 levels below (from Beginner to Master), read through the bullet points carefully. For each statement, rate yourself on a simple scale:

> **0:** Not yet

> **1:** Partially

> **2:** Fully

> (For example, if you fully agree with "I can introduce myself using simple phrases," give yourself a 2.)

2. Scoring

> Each level has 10 statements, so the maximum score for a level is 20.

> Add up your points for each level.

3. Determine Your Level

> ➢ Your current Confluent Level is defined by the highest level at which you score at least 50% (10 out of 20). In other words, if you score 10 or more at Level 3, you're functioning at least as an Emerging Speaker, even if your scores in higher levels are lower.

4. Reflect & Plan

> ➢ Look at the statements where you scored 0 or 1. These are your focus areas for improvement.

> ➢ Use the insights to adjust your practice routines based on the MKPF principles—work on your mindset, build relevant knowledge, practice regularly, and seek feedback.

5. Revisit Regularly

Set a schedule to retake this assessment every 6 to 12 months. Track your progress and see how your scores evolve over time.

The Confluent Speaker Fluency Levels (A1 – C2)

- **0:** Not yet

- **1:** Partially

- **2:** Fully

(For example, if you fully agree with "I can introduce myself using simple phrases," give yourself a 2.)

Level 1 – The Emerging Speaker (A1)

Statements	Only 0/1/2
I understand basic words and phrases but often hesitate to speak.	
I can recognize common expressions, but I rarely use them without help.	
I'm uncomfortable speaking, so I rely on gestures or silent communication.	
I rely heavily on translating from my native language.	
I need structured guidance to form even simple sentences.	
I struggle with pronunciation and often repeat words.	
I can introduce myself with a few basic details.	
I rely on memorized phrases rather than constructing sentences on my own.	
I often feel anxious about making mistakes.	
I can respond to very simple questions but find it hard to extend the conversation.	
Total score =	/20

My goal at this level: Start speaking, break the mental barrier, and build the courage for simple conversations.

Level 2 – The Expressive Beginner (A2)

Statements	Only 0/1/2
I can introduce myself and exchange simple greetings.	
I can ask and answer basic questions about personal details.	
I can describe everyday activities using short, simple sentences.	
I can use basic polite expressions without too much hesitation.	
I am beginning to understand the structure of simple conversations.	
I can express basic needs and wants, though I still make some errors.	
I can tell time and talk about basic likes and dislikes.	
I can handle simple social exchanges even if I need occasional support.	
I am starting to use memorized phrases in real conversations.	
I can respond to simple yes/no questions confidently.	
Total score =	/20

My goal at this level: Gain confidence in everyday conversations and move beyond short answers.

Level 3 – The Emerging Speaker (B1)

Statements	Only 0/1/2
I can engage in conversations on familiar topics with a fair amount of ease.	
I can express my ideas with increasing fluency, though I may still pause occasionally.	
I can construct more complex sentences than before.	
I start using a few idioms and familiar expressions naturally.	
I share personal experiences and opinions with growing confidence.	
I can talk about past events and future plans, even if I hesitate sometimes.	
I can describe events in a logical sequence during conversations.	
I participate actively in group discussions, even if I stumble occasionally.	
I have begun to use a wider range of vocabulary, though not always perfectly.	
I ask for clarification when needed and keep conversations going on familiar topics.	
Total score =	/20

My goal at this level: Develop a natural flow in conversation and reduce overthinking each word.

Level 4 – The Confluent Speaker (B2)

Statements	Only 0/1/2
I can maintain conversations on a variety of topics with relative ease.	
I articulate my ideas clearly even in more challenging discussions.	
I adapt my language to different settings, both formal and informal.	
I rarely need to translate; I start thinking in English naturally.	
I handle unexpected questions or topics without too much hesitation.	
I use idiomatic expressions and colloquial language comfortably.	
I actively seek and apply feedback to refine my pronunciation and clarity.	
I can participate confidently in debates and group conversations.	
I have a solid grasp of basic grammar and vocabulary as used in context.	
I can manage conversations that require sustained thought and connection.	
Total score =	/20
My goal at this level: Speak with clarity and confidence, using feedback to continuously improve.	

Level 5 – The Advanced Confluent Speaker (C1)

Statements	Only 0/1/2
I lead conversations on a broad range of subjects, offering unique insights.	
I can switch seamlessly between casual and professional English.	
I use advanced vocabulary and expressions naturally in my speech.	
I explain complex ideas in simple, relatable terms.	
I engage confidently in high-level discussions and presentations.	
I handle unexpected topics or questions with poise and clarity.	
I incorporate humor, storytelling, and examples to enrich my conversations.	
I adjust my speaking style based on constructive feedback regularly.	
I mentor others by sharing my insights and experiences.	
I communicate effectively in both formal and informal settings.	
Total score =	/20

My goal at this level: Inspire confidence and lead conversations that have a lasting impact.

Level 6 – The Master Confluent Speaker (C2)

Statements	Only 0/1/2
I speak with authenticity and authority that captivates any audience.	
I can effortlessly adapt my tone, style, and vocabulary to any context.	
I use idioms, metaphors, and cultural references seamlessly in my conversations.	
I lead complex discussions and debates with clarity and precision.	
I serve as a resource for others, offering guidance through my experience.	
I continuously refine my language skills through self-reflection and regular feedback.	
I embody a natural, confident speaking style that others look up to.	
I am recognized as a role model in communication and public speaking.	
I inspire and mentor peers with my clear, engaging language.	
I help others overcome their communication barriers through my example.	
Total score =	/20

My goal at this level: Own my voice completely and help others find theirs through my example.

Instructions for Your Confluent Score Game

1. Rate Yourself

➤ For each statement at every level, give yourself a score: 0 (Not yet), 1 (Partially), or 2 (Fully).

2. Score Each Level

➤ Each level has 10 statements, so the maximum score per level is 20 points.

3. Determine Your Current Level

➤ Your Confluent Level is the highest level where you score at least 50% (10/20) of the points.

➤ Also, note your overall percentage across all levels to see your broader progress.

4. Reflect

➤ Identify the statements where you scored low. These are your areas to focus on.

➤ Use the insights from the MKPF framework—Mindset, Knowledge, Practice, and Feedback—to plan your next steps.

5. Reassess Regularly

➤ Take this assessment every 6 to 12 months to track your progress.

➤ Watch your scores improve as you work on building your speaking confidence and fluency.

Final score counting across all levels

Level	Max Score (10 statements x 2)	Your Score	% Achieved
Level 1 – The Emerging Speaker (A1)	20		
Level 2 – The Expressive Beginner (A2)	20		
Level 3 – The Emerging Speaker (B1)	20		
Level 4 – The Confluent Speaker (B2)	20		
Level 5 – The Advanced Confluent Speaker (C1)	20		
Level 6 – The Master Confluent Speaker (C2)	20		
Overall Total	120		

Instructions

1. For each statement in each level, assign yourself 0, 1, or 2 points.

2. Sum up the points for each level and fill in the "Your Score" column.

3. Calculate the percentage by dividing your score by 20 and multiplying by 100.

4. Your current Confluent Level is the highest level where you achieve at least 50% (10 out of 20) of the points.

Use this table to track your progress over time. Revisit it every 6-12 months and see how your scores evolve as you continue to grow as a Confluent Speaker. Enjoy the journey!

Final Thought

Think of this Confluent Score as your personal game—a fun, ongoing challenge to help you see your growth. It's not about being perfect; it's about recognizing where you are now and celebrating your progress. Every time you score yourself, you're taking another step toward becoming the confident, fluent Confluent Speaker you're meant to be. Enjoy the journey, and let this game guide your continuous improvement.

> *When you focus on others' opinions, you lose your own voice.*

The end

www.ingramcontent.com/pod-product-compliance
Lightning Source LLC
Chambersburg PA
CBHW051237130726
47988CB00001B/384